ANTIQUE
PERSONAL
POSSESSIONS

ANTIQUE PERSONAL POSSESSIONS

SILVIA DRUITT

ILLUSTRATED BY MARY CAMIDGE & MARY SIMS

BLANDFORD PRESS
Poole   Dorset

First published in the U.K. 1980
by Blandford Press Ltd,
Link House, West Street,
Poole,
Dorset, BH15 1LL

British Library Cataloguing in Publication Data

Druitt, Silvia
 Antique personal possessions.
 1. Antiques – Great Britain
 I. Title
 745.1'0941   NK928

ISBN 0 7137 0925 1

Set in 11/13pt V.I.P. Plantin and printed in Great Britain by Fakenham
Press Limited, Fakenham, Norfolk

CONTENTS

INTRODUCTION

In writing of personal possessions in the nineteenth century it is inevitable that one should find oneself speaking almost entirely about the more privileged sections of society, as it was their possessions, in the main, which survived. Such possessions as belonged to the very poor were liable to be handed on and on, to the point of destruction. The many examples taken from periodicals and magazines reflect the same trend, less accentuated as the period progressed. These were mainly designed and written for the same people. The *Englishwoman's Domestic Magazine* was aimed considerably below the 'Top People'—none the less its readers were solidly middle class, mostly with leisure to perpetrate the embroidery designs on the needlework pages, and, at any rate, able to consider the models in the fashion plates. It is true that this magazine did, to a certain extent, cater for the impoverished (rather than 'the poor'); its exchange columns took advertisements from ladies offering to do needlework, lace-making and other genteel occupations at moderate prices.

Wars were almost endemic throughout the nineteenth century, but those which took place in Europe and the USA appear to have effected no very distinct long-term change in ways of life. It remained for the War to end War, and the War after that in 1939 to 1945, really to alter modes of life and, incidentally, to cause many of the productions considered within this book to vanish. But it is arguable that the greatest changes of all have happened within the last twenty years.

I have not attempted to make any comparisons between prices then and now. It should be remembered that a skilled Victorian artisan might make £3 a week, and raise a family on it, and that, in 1930, £300 to £500 a year was an excellent salary. Neither have I converted any prices into decimal currency; for those who do not remember, or who never knew:

One shilling (1s.) = 5p.; £1 = 20s.; 1s. = 12d.

[6]

1
TOILETRIES AND DRESSING TABLE

The Victorian woman at her dressing table, whether well-to-do lady with a personal maid or her less well-endowed sister, had at her disposal a very different selection of aids to beauty than her twentieth-century counterpart. In theory, at least, no open embellishment of the skin, by improving creams or colours, was supposed to occur—not for her, unless she were an actress or a whore (and to many at that time the terms were nearly synonymous), lipstick, rouge, eye-shadow or the like. In this she was more restricted than either her descendants, or her forebears in the eighteenth century and in Regency times, when Sir Walter Elliott could say of Lady Russell: 'If she would only rouge a little, she would not be afraid of being seen; but last time I called, I observed that the blinds were let down directly' (*Persuasion*: Jane Austen).

A Victorian therefore would have on her dressing table no great array of jars and bottles by a contemporary equivalent of Elizabeth Arden or other famous beauty specialist. The time of the great cosmeticians was still to come and any adventitious aids to beauty would be discreetly hidden away in a drawer, if used at all. Apart from moral disapproval by the Mrs Grundys, there were some grounds for the Victorian attitude to cosmetics: doubtless some of the ingredients were far from wholesome, and a knowledge of the havoc wrought by Ceruse (which contained white lead) in the eighteenth century would be reason enough! But that cosmetics were indeed used we shall see presently.

The modish pink and white complexion that was idealised in fashion plates of the time, could only, in all probability, have been enjoyed by a fortunate few whose skins could stand up to an ill-balanced diet (vitamins were unknown), tight lacing, and all too often a lack of fresh air and exercise; or by those who ignored the dictates of fashion and of corsetières, who, by inflicting fashionably tight corsets, deranged their clients' digestion and circulation, producing red noses and other ills.

In the absence of purchased cosmetics to cure or cover up complexion blemishes and artificially to heighten 'bloom' (and a 'brilliant' complexion was much admired, possibly because of its very rarity), many unacknowledged subterfuges were resorted to: for instance, fine oatmeal to reduce the greasy shine on a nose, geranium petals, rubbed on the cheeks and lips, which were said to impart some of their glowing colour, or lampblack* to darken eyebrows and lashes. It is, however, quite clear from women's magazines of the period, especially the advertisement and correspondence pages, that, in fact, very many women, not only actresses, were bent on improving their natural looks with enthusiasm. The *Englishwoman's Domestic Magazine* in July 1868 stated: 'It is quite plain that ladies are making much more use than they formerly did of a variety of applications for the heightening of their charms'. Even earlier, it reported that a M. Jozeau, of the Haymarket, London, would forward to enquirers a pure vegetable rouge; and in 1863 advertisements appeared in *The Queen* for Nisbett and Co.'s Damask Rose Drops, which are 'an elegant and innocent extract for giving instant and permanent colour to the cheek'. Mrs Lynn Linton in 1867, said: 'the girl of the period is a creature who dyes her hair and paints her face', habits of which it seems she disapproved; but Mrs Haweis found she could not totally condemn the practice—she was much in favour of the covering up of blemishes, which she considered more pardonable than the undiscriminating use of padding, bustles and false hair, and sometimes a kindness to the victim's friends: 'Let them let out their poor wasplike waists to something like a sane circumference, and evaporate with a spot of white the red spot on their nose'.

A tanned skin and freckles were to be avoided at all costs by those who wished to be considered either beauties or ladylike—it was only working women or countrywomen who would spend much time in the open air, so that the complexion it inevitably produced was an unfashionable one; just as, in the 1920s, a tan became fashionable almost as soon as Society discovered the beaches of the Riviera. In order to maintain or produce this fashionable pink and white complexion, parasols and bonnet veils were used, and a multitude of whitening creams and lotions, some from home recipes, such as this one 'from an old family receipt book' and recommended in the *Englishwoman's Domestic Magazine*: 'Take Alysson† seeds one part, two parts honey. Mix the above and apply to the Freckles as a pomatum. They will soon disappear' and 'Take half [a pint?] of milk with the juice of a lemon and a spoonful of pale brandy. Boil the whole and skim it clear of all scum. This is an infallible wash'. Some women, especially in the country, who still had the use of a still-room and the oppor-

---

* from the inside of a lamp chimney, or made by holding a saucer above a candle flame.
† presumably Sweet Alyssum (*Alyssum maritimum*).

[8]

tunity to gather fresh herbs, preferred to distil their own extracts and make up their own lotions from such well-tried home recipes.

Most of the lotions and creams, however, were bought from manufacturers or their retail agents or made up by apothecaries. One of the oldest was Gowland's, which is mentioned in *Persuasion* as having carried away Mrs Clay's freckles; though in 1868 a correspondent of the *Englishwoman's Domestic Magazine* found it 'Perfectly useless' when she tried to remove her daughter's sunburn. This lotion was still on sale during the 1920s. Rowland's Kalydor lotion, which was already well-known in the 1830s, was advocated in 1851, in the *Ladies' Cabinet* magazine, for:

'Ladies exposed to the scorching rays of the sun and heated particles of dust. . . . It promotes the healthy action of the microscopic vessels [of the skin], by which its general wellbeing and the beauty of its appearance are generally promoted. . . . Freckles, Tan, Spots, Pimples . . . fly before its application and give place to delicate smoothness and the glow of Beauty and of Bloom.'

This lotion was described as being composed of 'choice exotics of a balsamic nature' and in another advertisement as 'an Oriental Botanical preparation'. Many other preparations claimed, with or without justification, to be made from 'choice exotics', or oriental herbs, this advertising ploy still having its uses today, as has its counterpart, what might be called the 'English hedgerow' ploy. This also was used in Victorian times. Kalydor was still obtainable in the 1930s.

Among other lotions advertised for whitening the skin, Beetham's Glycerine and Cucumber lotion in 1886 'entirely removes and prevents all Sunburn, Tan, Redness . . . more effectively than any other preparation'. Glycerine was discovered in the eighteenth century, but its uses for skin preparations were not appreciated until the middle of the nineteenth, according to Eugene Rimmel in his *Book of Perfumes* in 1865. Beetham's Glycerine and Cucumber was so popular that in 1896 the makers changed the label, as the old one was being freely imitated:

'In consequence of the numerous imitations of their RED AND BLACK "GLYCERINE AND CUCUMBER" LABEL, Mr Beetham and Son have designed and adopted this new and distinctive one, which in future will be used both on the bottles and outside cases. It has been duly registered as a "Trade Mark" at home and abroad, and Mr Beetham and Son will be greatly obliged by any information regarding any imitations of the same which may be offered.'

This new label was in green, gold and chocolate. This lotion was still made in the 1920s and their Lait Larola, which had similar properties, from the late nineteenth century until at least the 1950s. Another old-established complexion lotion was the Lait Antéphélique made by Candès of Paris. In 1868 the agents for this in London were M. Jozeau and Corinne of the Strand. It was especially recommended for spots and pimples, and was another long-lived product, still advertised in 1926.

In addition to being good for female complexions, both Kalydor and Larola were strongly recommended as aftershave lotions.

Other whitening and soothing preparations included Godfrey's Extract of Elderflowers, Aspinall's Neigeline ('makes the skin like velvet'), and, for chapped and red hands, Marris's Almond Tablet which would make them white and smooth (c. 1890). So did Hinde's Honey and Almond Cream in the '20s, and it continued to do so until the 1950s.

In the *World of Fashion* of April 1891, Kaloderma was advertised as being superior to cold cream, lipsalve and vaseline: it was also said that 'detection is impossible'. This product, or one by the same name, was still popular in Europe in the 1930s, though in England Glymiel Jelly seems largely to have taken its place. They were both nearly transparent, colourless jellies and could not well have been other than undetectable. The statement probably reflects the fact that more and more women were in fact turning to salves, powders and other cosmetics, but still preferred to think that the hoped for improvement would be put down to nature. Trésors de Toilette, for instance, made a Crème Orientale which went on 'without any appearance of making up' and the 'exquisite Siamese Toilet Powder', which was described as imperceptible, must surely have been applied to a visible part of the anatomy! Already in 1868, Eugene Rimmel, the French perfumer who moved to London, was advertising Rose Leaf Powder (or Poudre de Feuilles de Roses) for the face and arms, and also Hebe Bloom Cream and Liquid Rose Bloom. The two first at least were still to be bought in the mid-1920s. Eugene Rimmel was perfumer to the Princess of Wales (later Queen Alexandra), and a man who well understood the power of advertising, as no doubt his frequent mentions in this book prove. Fresh novelties, from scented gloves and sachets to perfume fountains, were advertised in practically every number of *The Queen* and similar papers during the late 1860s and the '70s.

Powder compact in silver and enamel, from Fortnum & Mason 1935

The Poudre d'Amour by Picard Frères was not coy about its purpose either—it was 'a high class Toilet powder for the Complexion' and came in three tints, Blanche, Naturelle and Rachel, at 1s. a box. It was endorsed by Miss Violet Vanbrugh who found it very pleasant to use—of course, Miss Vanbrugh was an actress! In the very limited colour ranges obtainable then and up to the 1930s, one frequently finds the colour Rachel. This takes its name either from the actress of that name, or, more probably, from a certain Madame Rachel who set up a Salon in New Bond Street, London, in 1863, and had a great success. Alas for her many clients, most of whom wished to keep their visits dark, her most lucrative profession turned out to be a sideline in blackmail. After mulcting many, she ended her career as a beauty specialist in prison. By the end of the century, or even earlier, she would probably not have found so many victims to succumb to blackmail on such a subject, though 'undetectable' and 'invisible' were still terms widely used in advertisements. Rouge, as we have seen, had been in fairly common use for a good many years when, in 1923, Rouge Invisible Nildé was still claiming to be undetectable. How undetectable most kinds of rouge really were can be deduced from the remarks of that observant little girl, Daisy Ashford, whose heroine Ethel (in *The Young Visiters*, 1919) 'looked very beautiful and the dainty red ruge on her cheeks looked quite the thing'.

By 1900, and earlier, the realisation had dawned that there were very good profits to be made out of cosmetics and most, if not all, of the great perfume houses had ventured, to a greater or lesser extent, into this market. This increasingly important side-line in many cases became their chief enterprise. Not only Rimmel, but Yardley, Piver, Guerlain, Coty, and many others followed this trend and expanded their ranges to cover practically all aspects of make-up and toilet preparations. In the late nineteenth and early twentieth centuries, in addition to these, numerous houses specialising in beauty culture sprang up: Harriet Hubbard Ayer, Helena Rubinstein, Elizabeth Arden, Cyclax are names that spring to mind. Also, many chemists at this time were still dispensing their own lotions and creams. But by the 1920s making-up was spreading to all classes, cheaper brands encouraging a new and wider public to buy, not at expensive department stores or exclusive shops, but in markets and

Pot lid for Boots' Cold Cream, late 19th century

over the counters at Woolworth's after the sixpenny stores had opened. In these cheaper ranges two sorts of cream were sold mainly—cold cream and vanishing cream. The origins of cold cream go back a long way, to Galen in the second century A.D., and its name is due to the cooling effect it has on the skin; vanishing cream, first sold in the twentieth century, contained no grease and left a matt surface suitable for the application of powder.

Pond's Cold Cream and Vanishing Cream were among the best known—they were widely and cleverly advertised as being used and recommended by Society beauties and leaders of fashion:

'Pond's four steps to beauty are followed by social leaders of the world . . . Lady Violet Astor, Lady Louis Mountbatten, la Marquise de Polignac, Mrs Cornelius Vanderbilt, Jr . . . .'

The last of the four steps, the application of vanishing cream, was followed by powder. A scarlet lipstick, rouge, mascara and carefully plucked and pencilled eyebrows completed the picture. Most of the early twentieth-century face-powders were based on rice-powder, more or less fine according to quality, and the colour ranges were restricted—usually white, pink and Rachel; lipsticks in rose, red and cerise; but by 1925 Coty had already embarked on a very much wider range: nine shades of face-powder in twenty-one different perfumes, in boxes or compacts with their distinctive powder-puff design, and lip rouge, either stick or liquid, in seven colours. A less expensive but well-known lipstick was Tangee (which could be bought at Woolworth's). This was said to change its colour to accord with the wearer's complexion. Rouge and powder were also available in this range, which came from the USA.

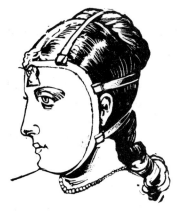

Madame A. T. Rowley's Toilet Mask, 1880s, as advertised in The Queen

As well as creams and cosmetics, face-masks were used for beautifying the complexion, for instance in the 1880s and '90s, Madame A. T. Rowley's 'Toilet Mask, or Face Gloves . . . a natural beautifier for bleaching and preserving the skin and removing complexional impurities'. This was a whole mask, with holes for eyes, nose and mouth, made of some soft and flexible material, possibly kid. What the beautifying agent was remains Madame Rowley's secret. Whole and part masks, and especially chin-straps for double chins, were used and sold by many beauty specialists, particularly from 1900 on, and many were patented. In 1924, Primrose House in New York used a system of 'Face Molding' and sold, as well as creams and tissue stimulants, a most uncomfortable looking Face and Neck Rest Strap. None of these, however, were supposed to do more than improve muscle tone or remove wrinkles. To flatten prominent ears or improve

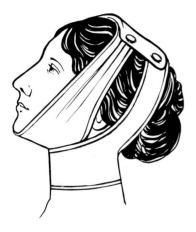

The Face and Neck Rest Strap, made by Primrose House, New York, in pink satin 1924

nose shape seems an altogether more ambitious claim, but this was what Claxton's Patent Earcap, in the 1890s, and C. Lees Ray's Nose Improver claimed to do. The latter was advertised for many years from the early twentieth century to the 1930s.

> 'Can any one tell me what will prevent superfluous hairs from growing on the face—something that will prevent them coming back without hurting the skin?'

This *cri de coeur* was answered by the advice to try the Poudre Juvenile invented by M. Jozeau (the agent for Lait Antéphélique), in 1869. 'Silkworm', the *Englishwoman's Domestic Magazine*'s equivalent to *Vogue*'s 'Shophound', said: 'Ladies need no longer have disfiguring marks or masculine appearance, for this "Poudre Juvenile" will restore their youthful feminine grace.' (Older ladies presumably were not supposed to worry.) Rimmel also made a depilatory, though it was not so widely advertised as his Rose Leaf Powder, Hebe Bloom or Perfume Fountains—more attractive items with immediate appeal! Neither depilatory was likely to effect a permanent cure and the users will have been just as disappointed as the users of the so-called 'Hair Colour Restorers'; when one reads that in 1919 the 'most popular, if not the most effectual' depilatory was one that contained orpiment (an arsenical compound, used in dyes and pigments), which could cause arsenic poisoning, and that another contained quicklime and pearl-ash, one cannot but agree with the correspondent some thirty years earlier who maintained that continued use was bad for the skin! In the twentieth century many more, and safer, creams became available and also small ladies' razors. In 1924, the Wonderstoen was produced in the USA—'Unwanted Hair whisked away by this dainty disk'. Dulcimo—the Magic Powder (c. 1910), which removed all odour from perspiration, was one of the first deodorants. This, however, claimed NOT to prevent perspiration; this was held to be unhealthy. Of course, back in the nineteenth century, true ladies, though they might 'glow', never perspired. One of the first toilet preparations actually designed to stop perspiration was the one with the expressive name of

[13]

Odo-Ro-No, which appeared in the 1920s.

Soap

Towards the end of the eighteenth century cleanliness began to be seen as a necessary part of agreeable social gatherings and, by Victorian times, had taken up its familiar position next to godliness. Improvements, except for the rich, in plumbing systems and hot water supplies were rather slow in keeping pace: bathrooms were by no means found in every middle-class household even in the 1920s. Good quality soap was, however, to be had much earlier than this, even if it had to be used at a bedroom wash-stand or in a hip-bath in front of the fire.

Andrew Pears, in 1798, produced a soap which, he claimed, had been 'purified of all noxious substances'. This was the beginning of the firm of A. and F. Pears who manufactured the famous transparent soap. Towards the end of the nineteenth century this was widely advertised; one of their most famous advertisements used Millais' painting *Bubbles*. In 1926 Pears announced with pride 'the greatest discovery in soap-making since 1798'—their Golden Glory soap, and it must have been not long after that the series of advertisements featuring little girls and headed 'How to become a beautiful lady' began.

In 1865, Eugene Rimmel wrote:

'The English toilet soaps are the very best which are made; the French soaps come next, but as they are not re-melted they never acquire the softness of ours. The greatest improvement effected in these preparations lately has been the introduction of glycerine. Although this substance was discovered in the last century it is only a few years since medical men fully recognized and appreciated its merits, and applied it to the cure of skin diseases. Another sort of transparent soap has been produced lately by incorporating glycerine in it in the proportion of about 1/3 to 2/3 glycerine.'

Unfortunately Rimmel does not tell us which brand of soap he is referring to, but before the end of the century there were many transparent glycerine soaps, some lavender-scented, and one, at least, transparent carbolic soap.

William Yardley took over a soap and perfumery business in 1801, but, as with most large-scale makers of soap at the time, his soaps were sold to retailers, who re-sold under their own names. It was not until 1900 that Yardley changed their policy and began to sell soap under their own brand name; but they did have a stand of perfumery and soap at the 1851 Great Exhibition, at which one of their exhibits was a cake of Brown Windsor Soap with a design of Windsor Castle moulded on it. The famous lavender seller, now associated with all Yardley's lavender products, was not used until 1919. She was adapted from Francis Wheatley's *Primrose Seller* in his *Cries of London* series.

The increasing importance attached to hygiene led to the production of various antiseptic soaps, which were much used in Victorian nurseries (and later). Wright's Coal Tar Soap, which in 1908 had already been 'prescribed by the medical profession for over forty years' was recommended as 'the Nursery Soap', and Lifebuoy Soap was said to be perfect for small babies.

The drying effect of most soaps on the skin was admitted, tacitly, by the very efforts which were made to overcome it by incorporating softening oils, such as palm or olive, cold cream, or lanolin. Messrs Field, who were also candle-makers, used spermaceti (from the unfortunate sperm whale, which also pro-vided sperm oil and ambergris), for one of their range—spermaceti also made some of the best candles. Palm and olive oils were combined in the famous Palmolive soap, from the 1880s, and it was advertised in the 1930s in a series on 'How to keep that schoolgirl complexion'. Among the more luxurious and highly scented soaps were already those of Roger and Gallet, including the still famous Sandalwood and Oeillet Carnation.

Shaving soaps were practically all made by firms already known for their toilet soaps and most of them were in the form of sticks. Pears Shaving Stick—'a shilling stick lasts twelve months'—was as transparent as their soap. Vinolia shaving soap was even better value, a sixpenny stick being said to last a year. Vinolia products were made by Blondeau of Paris; they also sold shaving soap in hand-painted vases and, by 1907, what appears to have been one of the earliest shaving creams in a 'collapsible tube'. J. B. Williams Co., who had their factories at Glastonbury, Connecticut, specialised in shaving soap. In 1890 they were producing, in addition to a shaving stick, a shaving tablet and a 'Luxury' shaving tablet.

Razors

Shaving soaps lead naturally to a consideration of razors and, for most of the nineteenth century, the only razor was the well-named old-fashioned 'cut throat', of which the best-known were the Kropp and the Wilkinson. They could be bought singly or in sets of up to seven—one for each day of the week, so as to be sure of a good blade. The Kropp Razor ('never needs grinding') came with a black handle at 5s. 6d. or an ivory one at 7s. 6d. in c. 1900, and the Kropp Duplex Graduating Strop could be used to keep a fine edge. When not in use the blade folded back into the handle. An expert hand was necessary to shave without cutting oneself and it must have been a terrifying experience to shave for the first time. No wonder so many men patronised barbers rather than tackle the job themselves, though it was possible to get a safety device that fitted on to the razor.

Many attempts to produce a safe razor in lieu of the dangerous open blade were made. One of the early ideas was to put a guard along the blade, as in the Patent Plantagenet Guard Razor, patented c. 1850 by Charles Stewart and Co. Hilliard and Chapman, in 1851, showed the 'Hypenetome, or beard plane, a new instrument for shaving on the principle of a carpenter's plane', which could be used either right- or left-handed. In 1880, the Kampfe Brothers patented

[15]

their razor in the USA. Of the Home Safety Razor made by Eastman and Krauss Razor Co. of New York (1891), it was said: 'Even if you have never shaved before, it is absolutely impossible to cut the face. It is especially adapted to the young just beginning to shave; to the old, with trembling hands. . . .' Other safety razors were the Midget (1893), marketed by Hovenden's, London, and the Roller Safety Shaver by Wilkinsons. Ironically, the great revolution in shaving came *via* a man who was not in the least interested in saving his fellow-men trouble or bloodshed; Gillette was only interested in making his own fortune by his invention of the thin, throw-away blade. But when, in 1903, after several years, the problems involved in producing a thin enough blade were solved, it became clear that this was indeed the answer. Not all men, however, threw away their old razors—in 1905 another safety device for the cut throat was patented. The next major change in shaving came with the invention of the Schick Electric Razor in 1931.

When the bathroom was ill-equipped or absent, it was absolutely necessary to have some sort of shaving-stand, with a mirror. More elaborate stands included not only a couple of bowls and a shaving-mug, but rests for brushes and brackets fitted for electric light or candles, as appropriate.

Shampoos

Hair washes were sold both by firms specialising in hair preparations and by general perfumers and soap manufacturers such as Vinolia, but it is often unclear whether a particular lotion is for cleaning the hair or for administering as a tonic to it. One of Mrs Beeton's recipes for a hair wash contains elder-flower water, vinegar, rum, glycerine and tincture of bark, and was for improving weak hair. More like a true shampoo is the German recipe calling for soft water, with bran and a little white soap, used with the yolk of an egg; but there seems to have been some reluctance to use soap on the hair, or at any rate to mention soap in connection with it. Several soapless recipes, such as borax, olive oil and boiling water, or rosemary water and borax, can be found. The most important recommendation is, usually, that soft or rain water be used. Probably most people did use some good soap followed by the application of a pomade.

By 1900, special shampoo powders were put up in tins or bottles and in the 1930s individual sachets appeared. A preparation called Stallax, resembling scrambled eggs in appearance, came in a tin and was especially recommended for children's hair. Evan Williams made a Paraphin Hairwash (paraffin was used as a stimulant) in about 1905, but the firm had a much greater success with, and became much better known for, their Tunisian Henna Shampoo, which added red lights to mousy hair, and their Chamomile Shampoo for blondes. At the beginning of the 1930s, for many girls, every 'Friday night' was 'Amami night', in preparation for going out on Saturday night to the 'flicks' or the Palais de Danse.

Dentifrices

An early recommendation, before the period under consideration, was to clean the teeth with the end of a wooden skewer, chewed till soft, when it would 'become the best and softest brush for the purpose' and every fortnight or so use a few grains of gunpowder, which would make your teeth 'of an inconceivable whiteness'. Home-made toothpastes and powders were still sometimes made in the 1860s—at any rate Mrs Beeton thought it worthwhile to include one of areca nut and ground cuttlefish bone. Another areca nut toothpaste on the market, from at least the 1880s to 1907, was made by W. Woods of Plymouth; it was recommended for 'removing Tartar and whitening the teeth without injuring the enamel' and, like almost all pastes, creams, and pomades of the nineteenth century, was put up in shallow white pots with the description on the lid. Judging by the numbers of surviving lids this must have been a very popular dentifrice. Those pastes which survived into the twentieth century changed to the more convenient tube.

Pot lid for Odonto, or Pearl Dentifrice, by Alexander Rowland and Son

One of the oldest toothpowders still available in the early twentieth century must have been Rowland's Odonto or Pearl Dentifrice—this was being made in the early 1800s and was compounded of the 'choicest and most recherché ingredients of the Oriental Herbal' (*Ladies' Cabinet*, 1851). It was still around in 1926—nearly all A. Rowland and Sons' products seem to have lasted well; this may be attributed either to their satisfactory effects or to fantastically high (for the time) advertising, which is said to have been £20,000 a year in the 1850s. An equally well-established dentifrice was Jewsbury and Brown's Oriental Toothpaste 'composed of pure ingredients medically approved and preserves the Teeth and Gums into Old Age'. It was in use from the early 1800s 'in the highest circles', not quite reaching the eminence of Odonto, which was said to be used 'by her Majesty the Queen, the Court and Royal Family, and Sovereigns and Nobility throughout Europe', all at 2s. 9d. a pot. Jewsbury's pot was eventually replaced by a tube—in the early 1900s both were available.

Pastes and powders were made of, and flavoured with, a variety of substances. As well as areca nut and cuttlefish, dentifrices were made with chlorate of potash, chalk, orris root, camphorated chalk—flavours could be rose, win-

[17]

'Crayon Rubens' Pencil
for Eyebrows and Eyelashes
c.1882

C. Lees Ray's
Nose Improver
c.1908-30

Claxton's Ear Cap
c.1898

Beetham's
Glycerine and
Cucumber Lotion
1893

Vinolia Powder for
Toilet and Nursery
c.1898

Bellin's Wonderstoen
Depilatory
1929-30

Poudre d'Amour
1891

Odo-Ro-No Deodorant
1930

Marris's Almond Tablet c.1880-90

[18]

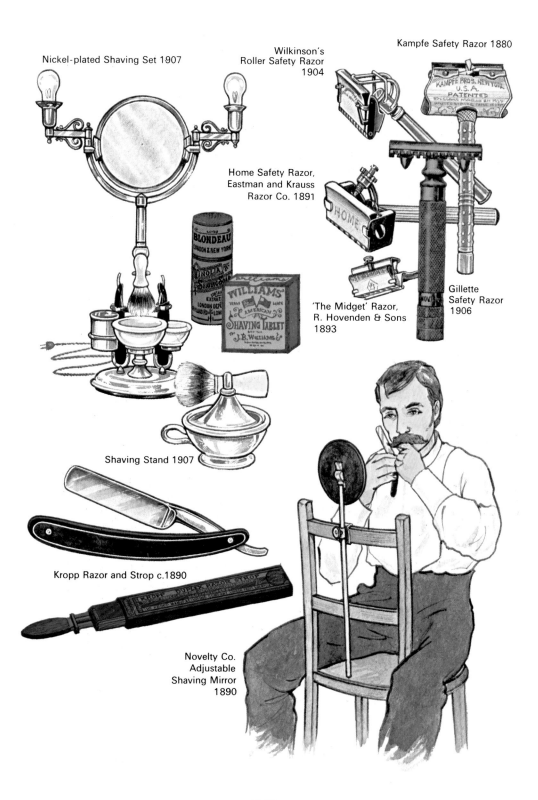

Nickel-plated Shaving Set 1907

Wilkinson's
Roller Safety Razor
1904

Kampfe Safety Razor 1880

Home Safety Razor,
Eastman and Krauss
Razor Co. 1891

'The Midget' Razor,
R. Hovenden & Sons
1893

Gillette
Safety Razor
1906

Shaving Stand 1907

Kropp Razor and Strop c.1890

Novelty Co.
Adjustable
Shaving Mirror
1890

[19]

tergreen, violet, cherry. Rimmel and John Gosnell made a Cherry Toothpaste in the 1850s, the second patronised by Queen Victoria. A lemon-flavoured toothpaste available until the 1950s was Genozo. In this respect we now have a much more restricted range, almost all toothpastes tasting of spearmint.

Antiseptic dentifrices included, in about 1900, King's Royal Antiseptic Tooth Powder in a round wooden box. Colgate's also claimed antiseptic properties. Forhan's 'for the gums' produced scare-raising advertisements in the 1920–30 period about pyorrhea ('Four out of Five' lose their teeth owing to it); Gibbs' Toothpaste advertising was addressed to children, calling teeth Ivory Castles and adjuring them to fight the Giant Decay. Liquid dentifrices included Dr Pierre's, first sold in the 1850s. Rose and violet mouth washes were recommended to sweeten the breath after smoking.

More orthodox toothbrushes were made even at the time when the chewed skewer was recommended, with bristles set in ivory, bone, or sometimes silver handles. Folding toothbrushes, with a leather case, were useful for travelling as they went easily into a pocket. Cases, as well as brush handles, were made of celluloid by about 1900. Dr Scott, who invented the Electric Hair Brush, invented a companion Electric Tooth Brush in about 1885.

Dressing

The basic requirements of the dressing table have changed little from age to age, ever since they have been known. Brushes, combs and mirrors now are quite recognisably the same objects as they were two hundred or more years ago. There were a few things, however, on the nineteenth-century dressing table which will now only rarely be found. One of these was a bonnet brush or whisk, a soft, long-bristled brush specially used for dusting hats and bonnets. There might also be a special brush for cleaning velvet—both of these would be likely to be *en suite* with the hair brushes and hand mirror. A ring stand, or ring tree, was used to hold the rings worn every day—the stand illustrated on page 22 is of Tunbridge ware, c. 1860 to 1870; though very valuable rings were more likely to be locked away in a jewel case.

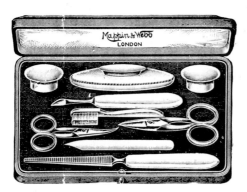

Manicure set by Mappin & Webb c. 1904

[20]

Pocket manicure outfit with red leather case, late 19th century

Dressing tables, as a rule, had one large oval mirror only, thereby setting a problem when complicated hairstyles had to be set to rights by anyone lacking a lady's maid. A mirror which could be fastened to the back of the dressing chair was a great help. This could be done with Dredge's Patent Mirror, in 1907, and with the almost identical mirror produced by the Novelty Co. of Birmingham some ten to fifteen years earlier.

In the mid-nineteenth century it was considered hardly decent for a woman to go out-of-doors unless wearing gloves, though it seems to have been permissible for a man merely to carry his, and many ladies even wore them indoors:

> 'In every costume but the most extreme negligé a lady cannot be said to be dressed except she is nicely and completely gloved; and this applies equally to morning, afternoon, dinner, and evening dress.' (Letter to *The Queen*, 1862.)

As it was also considered unladylike to be seen wearing soiled gloves, and as kid gloves were not washable, a good supply was always necessary to keep up appearances, though various cleaners were on the market, such as the 'Apokathartikon—the Magic Glove Cleaner, superior to benzine and camphine'. Those who could afford it bought their gloves in dozens and a glove box in which to keep them was almost essential. Even more so was a pair of glove stretchers, for easing tight new gloves; a glove-powderer—a wooden or ivory round box with a long, perforated nozzle from which powder was sprinkled into the gloves to help ease them on—and a small glove button-hook. Glove boxes could be long metal caskets, though the one illustrated is of leather and has an expanding base. A larger button-hook was used to do up button-boots, and boots and shoes were generally kept in good shape by wooden trees, which, with the more expensive footwear, were made to fit precisely into each pair. Hinged trees of the type illustrated were of more general use and, by the 1920s, folding metal shoe trees were used, especially practical for travelling as they were light and took up next to no room.

For most of the nineteenth century, clothes were hung up, not on coat-hangers (which then meant the small loops in the necks of coats to hang them by) but on pegs or hooks in the wardrobe. Mrs Haweis, in 1883, speaks of a garment 'when it is hung on a peg with no human form inside it'. It seems that it was not until the very end of the nineteenth century that coat-hangers in the modern sense were known—then called clothes-holders, or clothes-shoulders. The usual way of storing clothes until then was by laying flat, or by hanging from the aforesaid peg—Victorian wardrobes bear this out, as they have no rod

Bonnet Brush 1907

Tunbridge Ware
Ring Stand
1860-70

Silver Hatpin Stand
with Cushion
1905

Glove-powder Shaker,
2nd half of 19th century

Expanding Glove Box with Glove Stretcher and Buttonhook 1863

Shoe-trees by C. Benscheidt 1890-1903

The Crown Perfumery's
Old English Lavender Water Bottle
1901

Smelling-salts Bottle
c.1850-70

Double-ended Scent and
Smelling-salts Bottle c.1850

Cameo Glass
Scent Bottle
1894

Nailsea Glass
Scent Bottle
c.1860-70

Parfum Volt
Trade Card 1928

'Dans La Nuit',
by Worth 1930

4711 Eau de Cologne
c.1924

Chanel No. 5 1924

[23]

(or if they have it is a later addition) but a series of hooks around the sides; an early wardrobe trunk was fitted with two hooks, but, by 1901, a similar trunk had 'coats suspended on a rod by clothes-holders'. In 1897, something which appears to have been new was advertised in the *Sears, Roebuck Catalogue*: a 'wire coat or garment hanger, 17 inches. Garments when hung on this device do not lose their shape, as when hung on hook or nail'. These early hangers cost 45 cents a dozen.

Perfume and Perfume Bottles

Up to the 1920s, when deodorants first came on the market, scent played a much more important role in the toilette than it now does, although the truly 'refined' Victorian lady usually felt obliged to confine herself to Eau-de-Cologne, Lavender Water or similar preparations. The perfumer Eugene Rimmel himself had this to say on the subject, in his *Book of Perfumes* (1867):

> 'I should no more presume to dictate to a Lady which scent she should use, than I would to an epicure what wine he is to drink, yet I may say to the nervous: use simple extracts of flowers which can never hurt you, in preference to compounds which generally contain musk and other ingredients likely to affect the head. Above all, avoid strong, coarse perfumes and remember that if a woman's temper may be told from her handwriting, her good taste and breeding may as easily be ascertained by the perfume she wears. Whilst a lady charms us with the delicate aetherial fragrance she sheds around her, aspiring vulgarity will as surely betray itself by a mouchoir redolent of common perfumes.'

No wonder that Rimmel's perfumes were recommended in the *Englishwoman's Domestic Magazine* as the most ladylike; in fact this same magazine in 1871 gave recipes for distilling rose and lavender essences for oneself. There was, however, already a whole range of other, more sophisticated, scents, which were by no means simple flower extracts (though even these were not always necessarily what they seemed) and which yet could hardly be condemned as vulgar. Almost all the best stemmed from France.

Eau-de-Cologne, one of the oldest toilet waters to be still with us, was first brought to Cologne and manufactured there by an Italian, J. M. Farina, in the eighteenth century. Made to a secret formula, it was known as Aqua Mirabilis and owed its reputation to alleged medicinal properties rather than its virtues as a toilet water. Several drops to be taken in water were a palliative for headaches and other ills—ladies who in more recent years were accused of taking their Eau-de-Cologne as a stimulant were but following a well-trodden path.

The success of this cordial/toilet water stimulated a large number of competitors; among them F. Mühlens, who made a similar product, also in Cologne, which we now know under the trademark 4711. Many other firms later produced variants of this successful formula.

Lavender Water was the English speciality—lavender being one of the few scented herbs which grew strongly enough in England. It was first produced on a commercial scale by Yardley in 1824, together with lavender-scented soap. Among other manufacturers were Atkinson, Potter and Moore, Sprule, Maddocks, and the Crown Perfumery. Fields of lavender were at one time a common sight, especially at Mitcham in Surrey, where it was grown especially for this perfume. Nowadays Mitcham is almost entirely swallowed up in the suburbs of London and practically all lavender for scent is grown in France.

In the USA, the place of Lavender Water and Eau-de-Cologne was largely taken by Florida Water, which is said to have a fragrance somewhere between the two.

The Crown Perfumery, in 1901, produced an extra-special gift-casket in repoussé silver, with a cartouche for an inscription, holding one of their bottles of Lavender Water. Crown were also the makers, in 1888, of a 'delicious new perfume, Crab Apple Blossom'; although not one of the great or well-known perfumes, this must have been a popular scent and was still to be bought forty years later. Two flower scents which were greatly in demand during the nineteenth century and the start of the twentieth were Rose and Violet, not only for perfumes, but for flavouring and scenting dentifrices and other toilet articles. The odour of violets particularly was cherished at the end of this period and, in Edwardian times, hardly a manufacturer's list appeared without at least one violet-based perfume; Legrand's Oriza Perfumery in 1907 lists no fewer than five kinds of violet out of eleven different scents, Parma Violet being one of them. (Oriza also made scented pencils and tablets for stroking on the skin and keeping among clothes.) In 1912, the Violet Nurseries at Henfield, Sussex, were producing a range known as Allen-Browne's English Violet preparations; here violets grown, as it were, actually on the premises, appear to have been used, which was by no means always the case, since many perfumes, for a long time now, have usually been synthesised.

Cut-glass scent spray from Boots c. 1900

Before the development in the twentieth century of a specialised 'packaging' industry, it was usual for scent to be decanted from its original container into special ornamental scent bottles, perhaps forming part of the dressing table set.

[25]

Carmen Beauty Razor 1923

Pond's Cold Cream 1930

POND'S

EXTRACT SUPERS

COLD CREAM

Coty Compact 1926-27

Rimmel's Rose Leaf Powder
c.1900

POUDRE DE FEUILLES DE ROSE

OR ROSE LEAF POWDER

EUGENE RIMMEL

Tangee Powder and Lipstick

TANGEE

PAPIER
POUDRÉ

Papier Poudré 1920s

[26]

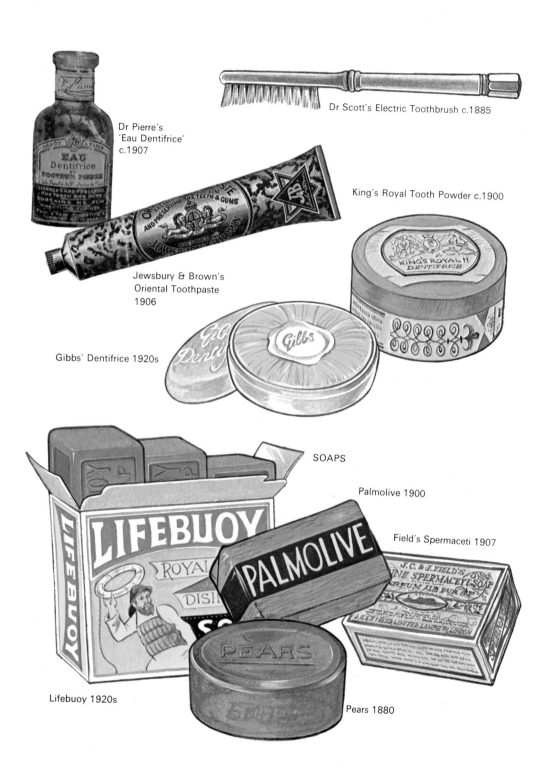

Dr Scott's Electric Toothbrush c.1885

Dr Pierre's 'Eau Dentifrice' c.1907

King's Royal Tooth Powder c.1900

Jewsbury & Brown's Oriental Toothpaste 1906

Gibbs' Dentifrice 1920s

SOAPS

Palmolive 1900

Field's Spermaceti 1907

Lifebuoy 1920s

Pears 1880

[27]

Other bottles were used in handbags, or for travelling, and smaller ones still were sold as châtelaine bottles, or to suspend from a fan so that the wearer could renew her perfume in the course of an evening. Small corkscrews, in dressing cases or attached to the neck of unopened bottles, were used in conjunction with a miniature funnel for the decanting process. A mid-nineteenth-century innovation was the double-ended scent bottle. Of clear red or dark 'Bristol' blue glass, this held perfume at one end and smelling-salts at the other—usually one end had a hinged, and the other a screw, top, both with a cork or ground glass stopper inside. A variant of this double-duty bottle from Rimmel was the following:

> 'For the opera-box there is an elegant ruby scent-bottle, containing perfume in a liquid form on one side, smelling-salts on the other. This bottle opens in the centre, and besides containing a vinaigrette, stands open and takes the form of an opera glass' (*Englishwoman's Domestic Magazine* 1869).

Many of these bottles were large and heavy, and appear awkward items to carry around in a reticule or handbag, but they do appear to have been so carried. Faceted glass bottles with red decoration, many from Bohemia, were used for either scent or smelling-salts—long, narrow, thick-walled bottles that held only a few drops of perfume may have been used for samples. Very beautiful cameo glass bottles were made by Thomas Webb and Co. of Stourbridge—the example illustrated on page 23 is probably one of theirs and its silver lid has the London hallmark for 1894.

Dressing table jars in cut-glass and silver 1909

By the early twentieth century high class perfumers began putting their scents each in its own highly distinctive bottle, which would remain as an advertisement for the firm. Coty commissioned René Lalique to design bottles for their range in 1910 and, in 1924, Mlle Chanel's scent, Chanel No. 5, was put up in elegantly simple bottles that have remained almost unchanged ever since. Unlike other perfumers, Chanel used the same bottles for her whole range. Guerlain, and most others, preferred a special design for each new perfume—the bottle for L'Heure Bleue, one of the most famous scents in the 1920s, is unlike any other in the Guerlain series. Worth was another who used different bottles for different scents—Dans la Nuit has an unmistakable bottle in deep sapphire blue with shining stars, eminently suited to its name.

[28]

Vinaigrettes and Smelling Bottles

These two were used for different purposes: the vinaigrette had originally been held to be a prophylactic against infection—in the late nineteenth and early twentieth centuries they were used for their refreshing odour, to counteract bad smells and relieve headaches. They contained a portion of sponge soaked in aromatic vinegar and usually consisted of a small silver oblong box, with a pierced inner lid, gilded so that the outer container was not affected by the acid.

A smelling bottle, on the other hand, was what was used to combat feelings of faintness and 'the vapours', to which so many Victorians are said to have been prone (though in the 1870s it was said they were going out of fashion!). They contained, not vinegar, but a pungent essence of ammonia with oil of lavender or other scent, with either a sponge or ammonium carbonate base.

A small glass bottle with a pierced metal underlid might have been either of these objects. With both, however, but particularly the smelling bottle, it was important to keep the lid tightly closed when not in use, to prevent evaporation.

Sachets

To keep the contents of her glove box, handkerchief drawer or wardrobe sweet smelling, the Victorian woman would use scented sachets. These were composed of orris root (the ground root of *Iris florentina*) with added ground flower petals and perfume. Perfumers also issued numbers of sachets, as advertisements, or sometimes forming part of a Valentine, in which case the contents might be merely cottonwool slightly impregnated with perfume.

Scented sachet of flower petal dust made by Marshall's, London Bridge c. 1900–20

The 'Princess' Fringe 1887

Plait and Curl for Chignon 1868

Dr Scott's Electric Hairbrush 1883

Batchelor's Instantaneous 'Columbian' Hair Dye 1863

Rowland's Macassar Oil 1902

'Imperial' Hair Waver 1862

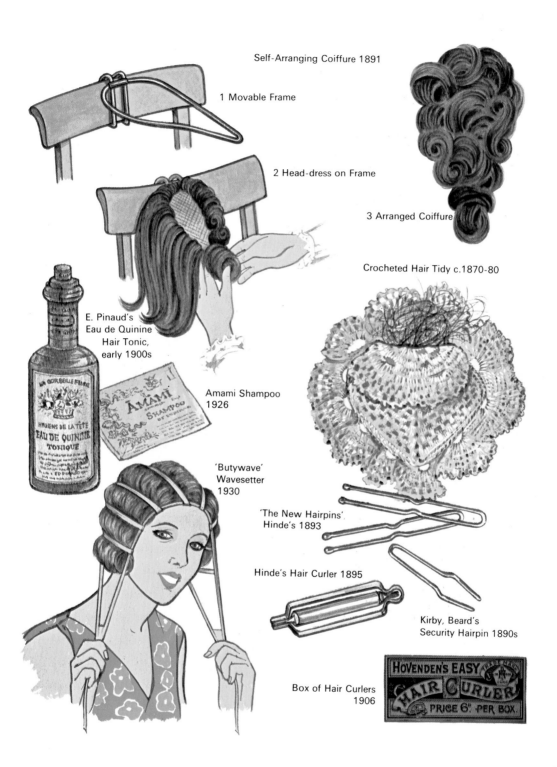

Self-Arranging Coiffure 1891

1 Movable Frame

2 Head-dress on Frame

3 Arranged Coiffure

Crocheted Hair Tidy c.1870-80

E. Pinaud's
Eau de Quinine
Hair Tonic,
early 1900s

Amami Shampoo
1926

'Butywave'
Wavesetter
1930

'The New Hairpins',
Hinde's 1893

Hinde's Hair Curler 1895

Kirby, Beard's
Security Hairpin 1890s

Box of Hair Curlers
1906

HOVENDEN'S EASY
HAIR CURLER
PRICE 6ᴰ PER BOX.

[31]

2
HAIR

One feature on which women liked to be able to pride themselves, and that could be cultivated without disapproval, was long and luxuriant tresses—many and various are the recipes for beautifying or strengthening washes and pomades 'to promote the growth of the hair' and, in the case of men, beard and moustache. As with complexion lotions, these could be home-made, from oils, rosemary and elder-flowers. As usual, Mrs Beeton is helpful on hair loss:

> 'Equal quantities of olive oil and spirit of rosemary; a few drops of oil of nutmeg. Mix the ingredients together, rub the roots of the hair every night with a little of this liniment, and the growth of it will very soon increase.'

However,

> 'When illness is the cause of the loss of hair, brandy should be applied three times a week, and cold cream on the alternate nights.'

Recipes for pomade include some based on lard, bone-marrow, or olive and castor oil. A lady writing to the *Englishwoman's Domestic Magazine*, on the other hand, recommended:

> 'To keep on and prevent the hair coming off: a few sprigs of box tree, boiled in water about an hour. When cold, wet the hair with the solution night and morning. In a week or two it will entirely prevent the hair coming off.'

Whether these home-made decoctions were effective or not, there was also a ready sale for a wide range of ready-made preparations. Bears' grease, a commodity much used by gentlemen (and ladies too) from the eighteenth century and earlier, was manufactured by J. and E. Atkinson from the early nineteenth century and also by other perfumers, amongst them, later, Eugene Rimmel. Bears' grease was still advertised in the early twentieth century, but though, in its earlier forms, it probably contained genuine bears' grease, later it appears to have been merely a name for pomades usually containing beef-marrow fat, lard or olive oil, variously scented.

Probably the most popular hair preparation of all time was the Macassar Oil made by Alexander Rowland and Sons of Hatton Garden, London. It was introduced in the early nineteenth century (or perhaps earlier) and became well-known, partly owing to extensive advertising. Rowland's were well ahead of the time in a just appreciation of the powers of advertisement and the Macassar Oil and other preparations were kept well before the public eye. A caution against 'unprincipled shopkeepers who vend the most spurious compounds under the same name' often formed part of the advertisement and some idea of the claims made for this oil can be obtained from this extract from *Bell's Weekly Messenger* in 1851:

'The following singular and authentic case of restoration of the human hair is worthy of observation, more particularly as it relates to an article of high and universal repute during the last half century. Mr. A. Herman, of Queen Street, Soho, had been quite bald for some time past, and had tried various preparations for the recovery of his hair, but without any beneficial result. He was then induced to try the effects of "Rowland's Macassar Oil", and after daily applying it for about two months, he, much to his gratification, had his hair quite restored, and now possesses a beautiful head of hair.'

Macassar Oil was recommended for women and children's hair as well as for men's, most of the illustrated advertisements depicting a girl with flowing hair. Owing to the greasy marks it made on chair backs, special washable covers were made, which are known to this day as antimacassars. It was still in use at least up to World War 2. The composition of the original oil remains a mystery; in the early nineteenth century it was described (not by Rowland and Son themselves) as being made of olive or almond oils, perfumed and coloured with alkanet. True macassar oil is obtained from a plant (*Schleichera trijuga*) which grows in the West Indies—Macassar is on Celebes.

Both the demure Victorian hairstyle with centre parting and ringlets and the exuberant coiffures of the late nineteenth and early twentieth centuries demanded a fixative or setting lotion that would hold the hair firmly. Again, Mrs Beeton has a recipe:

'1 oz gum tragacanth
¼ pt of cold water
3 pennyworth of essence of almonds
2 teaspoonsful of old rum.'

This has to be diluted for use and she adds that this bandoline actually improves the hair, instead of injuring it, which purchased articles may do. This type of fixative was in use still in the 1920s, but was slowly being replaced by spirit setting lotions.

Bandoline hair fixative from the Army & Navy Stores 1907

The later Victorian hairstyles demanded not only a fixative, but also a luxuriant growth of hair, and the many advertisements for hair tonics and restorers reflect the obsession of women who could never possibly grow a sufficiency of hair to meet the demands of fashion. In addition to the famous Macassar Oil, there was, in the 1860s, Mrs Allen's Hair Restorer, which 'contains the special aliment which is the life of the hair'. However, one user writing to a magazine had this to say: 'I do not think that anyone ought to use it that has ever taken mercury . . . upon the second application I found my teeth loose and mouth very sore. I took a little to a chemist, when he told me it contained the bichloride of mercury.' Needless to say Mrs Allen's representative strenuously denied this and an advertisement in *The Queen* in 1869 warns manufacturers against infringement of her trademarks. In the same year some of the more popular hair restorers were analysed by a commission set up by the *Chemist & Druggist* and the formula for Allen's restorer, at that time, did not contain mercury, so that the complainant may have been misled by an imitation. The claims for Allen's Restorer were certainly extensive enough: it was alleged to restore colour, arrest fall, remove dandruff, cleanse the scalp and renew growth. It was primarily a colour restorer, or slow-acting dye.

Other preparations are too numerous to do more than pick out a few. Rimmel's Lime Juice and Glycerine was first produced in 1864 and still available in 1925. This also had many imitators. Then there was Bay Rum, Eau de Quinine (the original inventor being E. Pinaud of Paris), Extracts of Rosemary (a centuries-old hair tonic), all of these being offered by several firms by the end of the nineteenth century. Among miracle-workers in the USA were the Benton Hairgrower, and Fechter's Famous Fairicon, 'a perfectly harmless Herb Remedy . . . not in a single instance has it failed'. Unlike many such remedies, however, it did recognise that there were limits to its powers and it was guaranteed to bring about new growth 'unless the roots of the hair be entirely dried up' (1880s). The Mexican Hair Restorer not only prevented the hair from falling off, but restored grey or white hair to its natural colour as well. It was not a Dye!

[34]

Advertisement for Harlene hair restorer 1893

One of the most popular hair lotions towards the end of the nineteenth century, and which was still going strong up to 1930, was Edwards' Harlene, a 'hair producer and restorer'. It was said to produce luxuriant hair, whiskers and moustaches, was a 'world renowned remedy for baldness and useful for restoring grey hair to its natural colour'. The advertisements certainly showed a positively abnormal growth of hair in humans and mermaids alike.

Only just second to the horror of losing one's hair was that of going grey and this also appears to have been a phobia common to both sexes. Dyeing one's hair was, apparently, if not more frequent, at least more acceptable than painting one's face. There were the slow-acting dyes, such as Allen's Restorer, and the Eau et Pommade de Laurier, which restored hair and beards to their natural colour 'without dyeing' and which was obtainable from Paris. There was also Madame Valery's Neolin Hairwash ('for infallibly restoring the natural colour'), Rossiter's hair wash (recommended in the *Englishwoman's Domestic Magazine*), F. E. Simeon's American Hair Restorer and, also from the USA, Wells' Hair Balsam. Complaints were made that the colour thus imparted grew out again—many customers seem to have been almost ludicrously credulous to be able to believe the exaggerated and impossible claims made for both hair tonics and colour restorers. Only a very few advertisers actually admit to any limit to their powers.

[35]

As well as restorers, there were the instantaneous dyes, used for beard and moustache as well. One of the best known in 1863 was Batchelor's Instantaneous Columbian Hair Dye. It had already

'an old-established reputation, and has proved itself the very best in existence. . . . It is instantaneous in effect; dies [sic] brown or black; and if the hair be nicely dressed with Churcher's Toilet Cream, it will be found to have succeeded in giving a perfectly natural effect.'

This was an American product: 'Each case is a New York original one, and is guaranteed to give satisfaction' or money will be refunded by the Agents, R. Hovenden and Sons, London. Churcher's Cream, also sold by Hovenden, 'imparts fragrance, richness and softness to the hair' and was sold in 'large handsome toilet jars, 1s., and in bottles for exportation, 1s. 6d.'. The dye cost from 4s. 6d. to 14s. a case.

By the 1890s the colour range was somewhat wider. Jean Stehr in 1891 opened 'special saloons for dyeing the hair' with a choice of forty shades, which would be good going even today; and in 1897 Broux's mixture was produced in 'twenty natural shades'. Mrs Haweis, writing in 1878, had already suggested that blue or green hair dye or hair powder would be a pretty fashion and to many faces most becoming—'if people whose hair is grey-brown can dye it chestnut, they might just as well dye it blue' but, in spite of this recommendation, blue rinses were not used until well on in the twentieth century. It is interesting to note that in 1907 the firm of Douglas included in their list of hair preparations five colours of hair dye, an 'electric' fluid, and gelatine. The beneficial effects of gelatine on the hair and nails have, it seems, been known for quite a long time.

In the 1870s to '90s there was a boom in electrical and magnetic contrivances of all kinds. Electricity was applied not only to industry and to mechanical devices, but pressed into service for health and beauty. In addition to magnetic, and allegedly health-giving, belts and corsets, means were found to apply it to

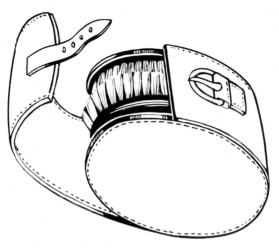

Pair of military hairbrushes in leather case 1930s

the scalp. The Electro-magnetic Curling Comb was supposed to encourage the hair to curl, but Dr Scott's Electric Hairbrush did more than that, being warranted to cure nervous and bilious headaches, neuralgia (in five minutes), and to arrest falling hair and premature greying. This was a bristle brush, and Dr Scott sternly warned against the use of 'so-called magnetic brushes' made of wire, as they injured the scalp and led to baldness. An earlier magnetic brush was referred to in the correspondence columns of the *Englishwoman's Domestic Magazine*, in 1870, by a correspondent who stated that 'Herring's Magnetic Brushes are of no avail'. Possibly these had the wire bristles so strongly disapproved of by Dr Scott. A so-called magnetic comb, with wavy teeth, was still available in the early 1930s and supposed to encourage a wave in otherwise straight hair.

Having tried, and failed, to achieve the necessary thickness or length of hair demanded by fashion, there was yet another way out—false hair, or even a wig. Possibly the nineteenth-century diet, possibly the effect of tight lacing on the circulation, or some other reason, had the effect of causing baldness. The many terrifying advertisements, illustrating not only bald men, but also almost totally hairless women, seem to indicate that this was a common worry. Mrs Haweis, too, says that sometimes extra tresses are more than an improvement 'they are a necessity; witness a very scanty supply of hair, or hair in patches, on a young head'. This sounds very much as though it was a not uncommon case, which she had frequently come across.

In the 1860s there was any quantity of false hair worn, as a large chignon at the back of the head, even by women with fairly good heads of hair. In 1868, according to *The Queen*:

'Chignons are increasing in size, and as they are likely to attain still more formidable proportions, attention has recently been turned to render them as light as possible, as few things produce a more disagreeable sensation than anything heavy on the head, and, besides, the heat produced . . . is most injurious to the growth of natural hair. The accompanying (illustrations) illustrate a new chignon which only weighs two ounces and a half. . . . We are indebted for the model to Mr Walter Truefitt, of No 1, New Bond Street, W.'

In the 1870s, there was, if possible, even more false hair, causing Mrs Haweis to exclaim:

'Within the limits of human growth it is admirable . . . beyond these limits beauty ceases and vulgarity reigns supreme! . . . huge plaits of three, stuffed and padded, mighty cables half as thick as one's arm that rise up aloft, rows of ringlets, which would require the whole head of hair to form them!'

It was quite an understood thing that false hair should be worn, especially on grand occasions. In 1863, already it was estimated that 100,000 lb of hair was sold in England, most of it bought from peasant women in France, and there was a chronic shortage of blonde hair. In 1868 fashionable plaited chignons and

[37]

curls were made up from ladies' own hair, to be sure of a good match. Combings would be saved up and sent off to be made up by, e.g. Messrs Stacey and Co., London—this is what all the innumerable little 'hair tidies' that survive are for, to hold combed-out hair for making into curls.

The Pompadour style, fashionable in the '90s and the early twentieth century, was usually raised up over pads to make the hair appear thicker and these 'rats', as they were called, were often made up of the wearer's own hair. In 1914 a classified advertisement in *Home Chat* announced the making up of switches and chignons on a 'new hygienic principle' from combings. During the fashion for large hats, c. 1890s to 1912, all this extra padding and hair made the necessary foundation into which hatpins could be skewered (see Chapter 3, *Accessories*).

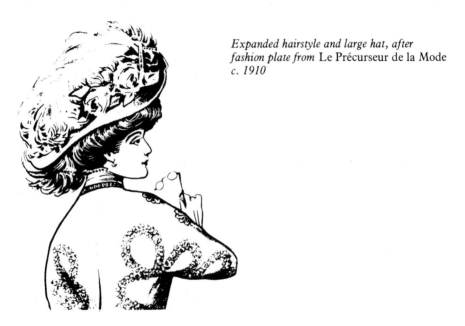

Expanded hairstyle and large hat, after fashion plate from Le Précurseur de la Mode *c. 1910*

In 1891, Wentworth Harrison of London designed the Self-arranging Coiffure, which must have been a blessing for those ladies unfortunate enough not to have personal maids, as it could be arranged in a convenient position in front of the would-be wearer, with no strain on the arms.

Unwin and Albert, with premises in Regent Street and at Belgrave Mansions, Pimlico, London, were a well-known firm for false hair as well as cosmetics. In the 1880s they advertised their Princess Fringe, 'an arrangement of curled or waved hair that can with facility be adapted to Ladies' front hair, quickly producing the present fashionable coiffure' (namely, the Alexandra fringe), and to keep it tidy Invisible Fringe Nets made of hair. Unwin and Albert were ornamental hairworkers to H.R.H. The Princess of Wales (later Queen Alexandra). In addition to fringes and curls they were able to supply 'perfectly

ARTIFICIAL EYEBROWS.

THE BEAU IDEAL of BEAUTY is well-defined eyebrows, the absence of them the greatest possible disfigurement. UNWIN and ALBERT supply artificially perfectly natural-looking eyebrows, 21s. the pair, forwarded on receipt of P.O.O. with colour desired.

Artificial eyebrows from Unwin & Albert, advertised in The Queen 1880

natural looking eyebrows'. No one at this time, however, seemed to have thought of, or at least advertised, false eyelashes, though the Crayon Rubens, made by F. Sobocinski near Leicester Square, London, when slightly touched over the eyebrows and eyelashes, gave 'BRILLIANCY, VIVACITY and power of FASCINATION to the eye'. This was available in all shades, price 2s. Unwin and Albert also did an eyebrow pencil and advised the use of Eastern Kohl. By Edwardian times they had added a third shop and they were selling what were now known as 'transformations' on the instalment system.

Most illustrations and portraits of the 1850–60 period showed women with a demure centre parting (very trying for some faces—there is a photograph of Baroness de Späth, in H. and A. Gernsheim's book *Fashion and Reality*, showing how a centre parting and dyed hair could make the worst of an unbeautiful face) and smooth glossy hair; but there were exceptions and, in the early 1860s, there were new fashionable ways of 'dressing the Hair', which involved waving and curling. The usual ways of achieving this were by means of plaiting, crimping with tongs, or curl-papers (even into the twentieth century, boxes labelled curling-papers were sold, the contents serving both for this purpose and as lavatory paper). A new gadget was patented in 1862, the Imperial Patent Hair Waver, which was said to have none of the objections that there were to the other methods. It was 'quick, easy and harmless', made of wood or 'a compounded metal substance', in a series of grooves into which another set, hinged to the first, fitted, thus pressing the hair into undulations. The whole was heated by means of hot water, and was supposed not to harm or break the hair as other kinds did. 'During the coming ball season, this invention cannot fail to become an indispensable desideratum to every lady's toilette' (*The Queen*, 8 November 1862).

The most usual method of curling was with hot curling-tongs, in spite of the danger of drying or even burning the hair. Curling-tongs were part of most women's dressing table equipment, and there were probably few households without a pair. Smaller folding tongs were available in the early twentieth century for travelling, and spirit-stoves for heating them. Unwin and Albert were advertising spirit-stoves in the 1880s, and also leather hair-curlers. To produce waves, 'crimping' irons were used, looking like multiple curling-tongs. However, in 1870, a certain M. Marcel Cateau, a young hairdresser in Paris, discovered the way to produce what became known as the Marcel Wave—entirely by accident, it appears, due to the tongs slipping in his hand

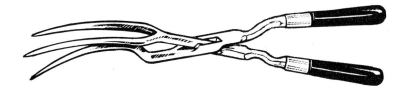

Double-pronged waving tongs c. 1900

when curling his mother's hair. This new method of waving quickly made his fortune, as many other hairdressers were keen to acquire this new skill. Marcel waving was especially popular in the 1920s with bobbed hair, but increasing use of water-waving and permanent waves in the 1930s, not to mention changes in fashion, almost ousted the hot irons method, for both waves and curls.

The practice of going to bed with the hair in curling-papers or other kinds of curler was imposed on many small girls and must have caused many sleepless nights, through the pain of curlers digging into the scalp. Better were the later metal curlers made by Hindes, which were used after wetting the hair, and being hollow helped it to dry rapidly. Best of all as regards comfort and ease of manipulation was the Butywave wave-setter of 1930. This was just put on over the damp hair and automatically pulled it into waves: 'no fuss, no bother, no gas, steam, electricity or hot irons'.

Long hair was general in the nineteenth century and those whose hair did not grow long usually helped it out with hair-pieces, as we have seen. To keep it up, many large hairpins, combs and bands were necessary. Victorian hairpins were generally long, straight and heavy, japanned black or brown. But in 1856 a Mr Edridge patented hairpins, in a variety of shapes, with corrugations which would not slide out so easily. They included many of the shapes obtainable recently, one of them having the same bends as the nowadays hard to find Witch hairpin. Hindes, in 1893, made the New Hairpin and Kirby, Beard, also in the 1890s, produced the Scientific and the Security.

More than hairpins were needed to keep up some of the hairstyles from the 1860s on. Making a virtue of necessity, some of the combs used for evening were extremely decorative. The large chignon needed a large comb to hold it in position, the most usual material being tortoiseshell, though ivory, bone and sometimes metal were used. The top of the comb was sometimes carved, set with polished steel studs, gilded or inlaid—the smaller comb shown on page 63 is hinged and the top is decorated in piqué. Black combs, of jet or with jet tops were worn for mourning. Sometimes several matching combs would be necessary. Double-pronged pins of real or imitation tortoiseshell were also used, but single or double pins with a jet star or, perhaps, butterfly in cut steel studs were mostly purely ornamental and fulfilled no useful function in keeping up the hair.

3
ACCESSORIES

Jewellery

The young Victorian girl in the 1860s was advised not to wear any but the simplest jewellery and to leave diamonds and other precious stones to her elders. In the daytime, a gold chain and locket, or a pocket watch on a fine gold chain were considered suitable, both in England and the USA, where Katy and Clover Carr received just such a gift from their Papa one Christmas (*What Katy did at School*: Susan Coolidge, 1870). For evening wear a pearl necklet and bracelet were most suitable and semi-precious stones, such as turquoise and coral, also acceptable; but fresh flowers were regarded as the best possible ornament for a girl. For a ball, she would carry a small bouquet, given by an admirer (if she had one)—these bouquets were small formal arrangements with a lace-paper surround and were carried in a bouquet holder, vase-shaped or sometimes resembling a small cornucopia, and made of pinchbeck or silver filigree. Some holders had a chain attached, with at one end a finger ring and at the other a pin, so that the bouquet could be fastened to the gown for convenience; as the dear girl would probably be carrying a fan, a dance programme and a lace-edged handkerchief as well, some such arrangement was necessary. The Magic Bouquet Holder, advertised in 1873 by Lionel and Alfred Pyke, of Ely Place, Holborn, London, had the advantage that 'when not in use, by simply touching a spring, the holder is converted into a stand for the table' by putting out three legs—in imitation gold or silver this cost 7s. 6d. A flower holder of a different type was the Butterfly Floral Brooch. This was more expensive than the 'Magic' holder, being made of silver-gilt at 1 guinea or of gold at 3 guineas: the body of the butterfly formed a small receptacle for one or two flowers. (A later, and invisible, holder was a glass or silver tube hidden behind a man's lapel to keep a buttonhole flower fresh all day.) Fresh flower wreaths, for evening, 'are the most perfect, and the least appreciated', and were often replaced by

[41]

artificial flowers, sometimes of wax—'of course, the excuse will be that in a hot room real flowers tumble to pieces. The answer is—'Not if you choose the right ones', said Mrs Haweis in 1878, and proceeded to list some which will last out a day and a night. One of the advantages of real flowers was their scent: the Paris correspondent of *La Belle Assemblée* (an English magazine) wrote early in 1858:

'Perfumes are scarcely required this month; bouquets are nearly all of real flowers, and the Violets and their odour predominate.'

Sentimental and Mourning jewellery is one of the things that spring first to mind when thinking of Victorian attitudes, but it was known well before then. Hair had been used in ornaments since the early eighteenth century at least, though it did receive a new impetus in the 1850s. Hair jewellery is associated nowadays almost entirely with mourning, conjuring up an instant vision of ghoulish relatives gathered round, waiting for the moment to snip off the hair of a dying person; but though much hair jewellery is in memory of a dead relative or friend, it is a mistake to assume that all of it is. A lock of hair had been a favourite keepsake for a long time and it is probably almost as often a lover's, husband's, sister's, daughter's hair that was made up into a chain, bracelet or locket, while the original owner of the hair was still very much alive. It need not indeed have been a sweetheart or very close friend—Emily Eden (*Letters*) records that, when in 1835 her brother left for India to become Governor-General, he was nearly bald from giving away locks of hair to his many friends and acquaintances.

A long necklet made of the hair of five sisters, joined by gold clasps, is likely to be of this kind, like that promised by Bella Wilfer to her Pa (in *Our Mutual Friend:* Charles Dickens). And in *Sense and Sensibility* by Jane Austen, Edward Ferrars was suspected, wrongly, of having snitched a lock of Eleanor Dashwood's hair to put into a ring.

On the other hand, a brooch (or other ornament) with hair forming a weeping willow, or with black enamel and pearls (standing for tears), is unmistakably a mourning brooch. Even more conclusively, they often bear the words 'in memoriam' or an engraved name and date of death.

As well as brooches and rings displaying hair, there were also those that kept it hidden from sight, as in a locket. This was undoubtedly best, whether for mourning or love token, when the hair was arranged by an amateur, as it frequently looked untidy, and chains and bracelets easily grew shaggy and objectionable from much use. It was better to have it done professionally, as by Mr Dewney in 1847.

'To Ladies wishing to preserve the Hair of a Relative or Friend, Mr Dewney wishes to state that he is a Working Artist and that hair entrusted to him does not leave his possession until made and returned in the form devised. An elegant Hair and Gold Ring 3s. 6d; fine guard ditto 5s. 6d' [i.e. A watchguard or chain]

[42]

and in 1852 appears an advertisement for hair rings:

> 'lined throughout with good solid gold and two hearts united upon it, with initials'.

These are 7s. 6d. and sound very much more like love tokens than mourning rings.

As mentioned above, hair chains and bracelets were likely to become worn and dirty, and a correspondent in *The Queen* in 1862 asked for the correct method of cleaning them. Another reader obliged with a continental recipe for washing in borax, first removing all metal parts. A lock of hair kept hidden in a locket—gold with a central star of pearls and turquoise was favoured, or gold with black enamel—was not so prone to this danger. However, later, when photography became common, it was found that a small photograph in the locket (or in a silver frame on the mantelpiece!) was even more evocative of the loved one, whether dead or only temporarily absent, and it would replace, or be added to, the treasured lock. Some brooches, often large and heavy, were made with reversible central frames holding hair on one side and a photograph or daguerrotype on the other.

In addition to rings or brooches bought spontaneously as mementos, it was not unusual for the deceased to leave in his or her Will a sum for the specific purchase of mourning jewellery.

Widows were particularly hard done by, in respect of jewels, by what one can only call the Victorian passion for mourning, which was, if not caused, at least encouraged by Queen Victoria's refusal to put off her mourning for the Prince Consort. This ill wind, however, at least blew some good to the makers of Whitby jet jewellery. The dull gloss of real jet was eminently suitable for wear with the heavy crape-trimmed dresses and *Sylvia's Home Journal* in 1881 stated that jet ornaments were the only ones permissible in the first year of mourning. Necklaces, earrings, carved brooches and bracelets found a ready sale, especially after the Great Exhibition of 1851, where a stand was devoted to this craft. The designs were sometimes finely carved but usually set on a heavy foundation, so that bracelets appeared more like fetters than jewellery; and watch chains can only be described as massive. The flourishing industry which grew up only lasted a few years. Soon after the time of 'Sylvia's' pronouncement, excessive mourning had already ceased to have quite its old importance, being felt more and more as an imposition and expense. Also, the rather expensive real jet was to a great extent ousted by 'French jet', which was in fact glass. Though black, it had a more brilliant gloss than Whitby jet and faceted beads made quite a sparkling effect as chokers, or strung on elastic for bracelets. It was also very popular for earrings, smaller and more elegant than most of those made of true jet. 'Paris jet is only worn for slight mourning' (1871).

Another form of sentimental, though not mourning, jewellery was the message, love, or name brooch, usually inexpensive, and of silver, in shapes or with

[43]

stamped-on designs symbolic of hope, love, remembrance and so forth, or bearing the name of the recipient. Mementos of this kind could be of places as well as people and silver brooches (usually in a 'knot' shape), set with a thistle, may be reminders of a visit to Scotland. Scottish cairngorms, set in gold or pinchbeck, were not strictly mementos, but without a doubt owed their popularity partly to Queen Victoria's devotion to all things Scottish.

Cameos, fashionable in the Regency period, were almost equally so in the middle of the century and after; a general hankering after antique forms was evident in jewellery, whether classical, mediaeval or cinquecento, either in gold with precious stones, or in cheaper metals with enamel. Pendants, brooches and earrings with attached drops depending from chains were much worn, as well as large cabochon stones in heavy gold settings. For those who wanted diamonds but who could not afford them, paste formed an increasingly good substitute; at the Paris Exhibition of 1878 the so-called Diamanté Brilliants, said to be indistinguishable from real diamonds except by an expert, attracted much notice and were introduced into England by Thornhill's in 1880. There was also the Orientoid pearl sold by V. Givry of Old Bond Street, London, 'equal to, if not rivalling' the real pearl. For settings, the improvements in electroplating meant that silver could often be replaced by plated metal and Abyssinian Gold Jewellery, made by L. and A. Pyke in 1873, was 'the only Imitation equal in appearance to 18-carat Gold', but nevertheless only one of many.

In addition to these ornaments in traditional shapes there were many short-lived novelty fashions in jewellery. Such a one in 1880 was Messrs Thornhill's Mouse or Pig jewellery in 18-carat gold or in silver. A woman buying a Mouse set would have two silver (or gold) mice dangling from her ears by their tails, another five or six crawling round her neck, and bracelet and brooch to match. This was described by *Le Follet* as 'the fashionable eccentricity of the day'. Another eccentricity, from the same firm, was silver anklets with bells on, presumably derived from oriental dancers—one cannot really imagine the truly 'refined Victorian lady' wearing these!

Small insect, bird, reptile or animal brooches, of a less startling kind, were, however, constantly popular right up to the 1930s (and are in fact still advertised). Victorian Bee brooches, of amethyst and other gems set in gold, and Art Nouveau dragonflies with wings of enamel, are on the whole much more attractive than the diamond-studded grouse or scotch terriers of the 1920s; in the 1930s, Woolworth's threepenny and sixpenny counters also yielded costume jewellery sporting animal motifs—for instance, a brass lizard brooch, similar in design, if not in materials, to Victorian lizard brooches. They also sold small Scottie brooches in highly polished faceted metal, resembling the diamond-studded ones at Asprey's in appearance, though not in price. For men, the animal influence in the nineteenth century and later, was chiefly

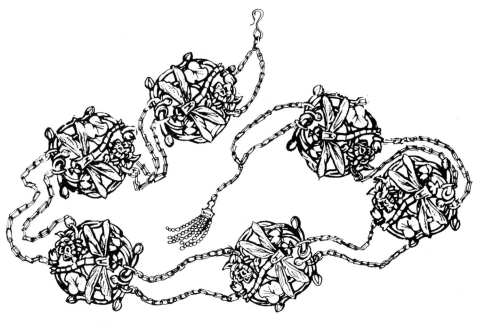

*Art Nouveau belt. White metal plaques cast in typical
dragonfly design c. 1890–1910.*

confined to those connected with sport; tie pins carried fox masks, horseshoes
or hounds, especially suitable for sportsmen but by no means restricted to
them.

One other form of hair jewellery appeared in the 1920s—that made of
elephant hair, usually rings or bangles. This was supposed to bring luck to the
wearer—I have not been able to trace the origin of this superstition, but it
certainly brought no luck to the elephants.

Earrings, up to the mid-1860s, necessarily meant pierced ears, an operation
that put off many women. Meg, in *Little Women* (Louisa Alcott), had earrings
tied on with cotton, but this was on the, to her, rare occasion of a party, and
must have been a rather insecure makeshift. But in 1866 Mr G. Searle, a
goldsmith of Plymouth, patented a design for 'earrings without piercing the
Ears!', which, he claimed, were 'most elegant appendages'. Several correspon-
dents wrote to the *Englishwoman's Domestic Magazine* in praise of these earrings; one, calling herself Daisy, said: 'I am happy to inform you that I have for
the last twelve months had Mr Searle's Patent Earrings in constant use and have
found them everything that could be wished. . . . I should also say that with the
top you can wear any drop you please.' Another reader had worn them some
time and found them very comfortable—'also the screws less perceptible than
in another patent'. Searle's earrings consisted of two bent wires holding a flat
metal disc on either side of the earlobe. The round body of the earring, on the
front wire, had a screw through it, which by acting on the back wire tightened
the discs on the ear. Earrings to screw directly on to the ear were an invention of
1899, though not really frequent until the '20s. After the heavy mourning

[45]

earrings in jet and the long, gold ones with multiple drops after 'antique' styles, most early twentieth-century earrings were mere diamond or pearl studs, until after the 1914–18 war. Then, when hair was first bobbed, then shingled or even Eton-cropped, ears came into their own again and all the space between earlobe and shoulders was available for decoration in the evening. Long straight drop earrings, of pearls, crystal, jade, onyx or other stones, filled this gap and the straight downward line (this was the time of no busts or waists, remember!) was further carried on by long necklaces of artificial pearls or other beads to match. For by now good artificial pearls were being produced, by Ciro, Tekla, and other firms. And what was even more, the great Mlle Chanel, the Paris couturier, had made blatantly artificial costume jewellery not merely acceptable, but positively fashionable. The sparkling blue glass and paste clip illustrated on page 51 was made in France and worn at the base of the décolleté back of a sapphire blue satin evening gown of 1932.

Jewellery for men, within our period, was somewhat more limited, though in the '50s and '60s, especially in evening dress, there was more latitude and a man might be gorgeous to behold, with diamond studs, gold chains, and brilliant cuff links. Later, this was regarded as 'vulgar display', and caricatured in *Punch* (1880) in the person of the *nouveau-riche* Sir Midas. However, tie pins, cuff links, rings (often signet rings) and above all the watch chain, all gave ample opportunity for the embellishment of the Victorian male. Any of these items could be either inconspicuously 'in good taste', or showy, and a heavy gold watch chain with seals might be worn by a man who would have scorned any other form of jewellery. A watch chain could be hung with seals, silver pencil cases, miniature compass and other trinkets until it almost resembled a woman's charm bracelet. Tie pins could have a modest enamelled top, or blaze with diamonds. In the 1920s and '30s cuff links were inconspicuous, gold or silver, engine-turned and sometimes with enamel decoration. Pearl studs for evening were the rule.

Hatpins

Bonnets were kept on by their ribbons, small hats could be anchored by small, unobtrusive pins. It was not until hats began to grow really large that the fashion for decorative pins came in, though somewhat similar pins had been used only decoratively in head dresses of the 1820s and '30s.

Hats began to grow in the '90s, with high trimmings of ribbons and flowers, fur and especially feathers. During the first decade of the twentieth century they increased until by 1910 they resembled huge mushroom-shaped extinguishers. Two things were necessary to wear these gigantic creations; an expanded hairstyle puffed out with pads (see Chapter 2, *Hair*) to hold up the hat, so that the wearer was not totally eclipsed, and large hatpins to anchor it firmly. The larger the hat, the longer the pin tended to be, and some were so long and sharp that there was controversy in many places about their dangers. There was an embargo in Berlin on excessively long, unguarded hatpins, as the result of an incident when a woman lost an eye and, in April 1913, the *New York Times* published a letter about a man who contracted blood poisoning from a wound inflicted by one of these dangerous weapons. Many of the longer and more ornamental thereafter were fitted with a safety knob.

Some of these pins were very highly ornamental, with decorative tops of jet, silver, mother-of-pearl and in an innumerable variety of shapes. The ones illustrated on page 55 have matching buttons, in two colours of shell, and their own velvet-lined case. Silver, thistle-topped pins were probably souvenirs from Scotland. Ordinary black-knobbed pins were bought in packets. These survived after the long, decorative hatpins had vanished from the fashion scene with the passing of large hats; they continued to be worn by unfashionable women who had not had their hair bobbed and did not wear cloche hats. A few ornamental pins were to be seen on hats in the 1930s, but these were purely for decoration and did not fix the hat to the hair.

Fans

At the beginning of this chapter, we left a Victorian girl at a ball, clutching her bouquet, her embroidered handkerchief, her dance programme and a fan—and only two hands for the four. Probably the one she could least have done without was the fan. Although the heating in most houses might be, if not inadequate, at least patchy, the tight and yet voluminous clothing that women wore made the fan a most useful accessory in winter and an absolute necessity in summer, to cool down a face flushed by overheating, exercise or dining too well. Lighting by gas, oil or candles generated far more heat than electric light and a large assembly, lit by any of the three (but especially candles, as so many were needed) would become insufferably warm.

The increasing volume and weight of dresses, especially the sheath-like fitted gowns of 1880, may have had a good deal to do with the much larger size in fans, as the ability to stir up a good draught was not so essential with the thin muslins and silks of the early nineteenth century (even though these may not have always been as easy and comfortable as they look). A lady was not supposed to perspire—this may have been the reason why men, at least as warmly clad, appear not to have felt the need for fans at this time. Another factor was probably that heavier skirts and richer ornament would have eclipsed any but a large and showy fan.

Fans used by day were of course relatively simple and small—in the middle years of the century they were often wooden Brisé fans, that is, fans without a leaf, consisting of carved and pierced sticks joined by ribbon. Duvelleroy, the largest maker of fans, of Paris and London, and Rimmel, the perfumer, both made fans of this kind and some which could be handpainted by the purchaser

Ivory brisé fan of very unusual shape c. 1860s

to her own design. Rimmel in 1868 advertised 'The New Initial Fan, ornamented with a Floral Letter. In whitewood 2s 6d, enamelled 5s.' and also 'Parisian and Viennese Fans in great variety'. Piver, another Parisian perfumer with a shop in Regent Street, London, was also known as a stockist of French fans—and, in fact, English fans seem to have been held in rather poor esteem. Paper or silk parasol fans, which opened into a full circle, were used by day (one can be seen illustrated in *The Empty Purse* by J. Collinson) and, in the late '60s to the '80s, Dagger fans, with metal hilt and leather or velvet sheath, were worn suspended from the belt.

According to the Paris fashion correspondent of *La Belle Assemblée* in the spring of 1858, 'the most fashionable Fan has a lace leaf', and this was a fashion which persisted until after 1900. Black or white silk fans with glittering steel spangles, often in swagged designs, were modish in the 1860s. These were medium-sized, but were followed by very much larger fans—many are depicted by G. du Maurier in *Punch* during the '80s, some of them extravagantly huge. Feathers were the rage—up to sixteen large curled ostrich feathers to a fan with tortoiseshell or mother-of-pearl sticks. Another favourite fan (from Paris) was the circular 'gigantic' fan of swansdown with a whole stuffed bird in the centre—a variant of this, advertised by Liberty in 1880, was a circle of peacock feathers and obviously designed to wear with 'aesthetic' dresses.

In general, much havoc was wrought among the more exotic birds, especially humming-birds, to trim hats, muffs, fans and other articles of dress—not only birds were used, but also many kinds of insect and small animals, including kittens, to 'ornament' dresses and accessories. Among the more revolting objects of this kind were earrings formed of humming-bird heads.

In marked contrast to the large fans above, were the so-called Empire fans in imitation of the early nineteenth-century style; small fans of this kind were used from the late '90s and into the '20s, when they might be carried inside an evening bag. But on the whole, after World War 1, fans were only still seen as large presentation fans, carried by débutantes—except for the small, cheap paper fans, advertising restaurants and hotels, which were provided by

[48]

thoughtful managements to cool down ladies who no longer carried their own.

Visiting Cards and Card Cases

The ceremony of 'leaving Cards' was an important part of Victorian and Edwardian Society's ('Society' with a capital S) etiquette of paying 'morning calls', which actually took place in the afternoon ('after luncheon, morning calls and visits may be made') or on other occasions, such as visits of condolence.

> 'In all visits, if your acquaintance or friend be not at home, a card should be left. The form of words "Not at home" may be understood in different senses, but the only courteous way is to receive them as perfectly true. . . . In making a first call, either upon a newly married couple or persons newly arrived in the neighbourhood a lady should leave her husband's card with her own.'

Mrs Beeton, quoted above, has either made a slip, or a slightly different set of rules obtained in her *milieu*—according to Charles Dickens (see again *Our Mutual Friend*) and others, two of the husband's cards should be left, one for each of the couple visited. A lady never left her card on a gentleman, so that one of hers sufficed. If there were other adult members of the family, of course the matter was more complicated. A card, or cards, would likewise be left to condole, when it would be marked 'p.c.' (*pour condoler*); after an entertainment, marked 'p.r.' (*pour remercier*), or before any long absence, marked 'p.p.c.' (*pour prendre congé*). A corner turned down meant that the card was left in person and not by deputy.

Men's cards were customarily smaller than women's, and with smaller cases, so as to go easily into a pocket. Some women's cases were quite large and heavy, especially the carved ivory ones; many remain today in perfect condition, so that one cannot but suspect that they were not a great deal used, but discarded in favour of some lighter and more utilitarian container. The materials used were chiefly ivory, sandalwood, silver or other metals, mother-of-pearl, tortoiseshell and lacquer, either singly or in combination. Perhaps the most common was the case panelled in mother-of-pearl, sometimes engraved, or with borders of darker shell. The earliest type had a lid which slid on, a shape which was used throughout. From the middle of the century, however, a case was favoured which had a hinged lid, but as the hinge was on the narrow edge it frequently broke and was not really successful, except with metal cases. A later type opened like a book, with hinges all along one side, and these usually had pockets to hold the cards. A curved silver case without a lid was a late nineteenth- and early twentieth-century favourite with men—it fitted into the breastpocket without making bulges or showing sharp corners. For a woman, it was really more economical of space to use one of the cases which was a combined card and money holder.

Card cases were among the many things that were sold as souvenirs at seaside and other resorts—mostly produced in Scotland by Smith of Mauchline and

Fur Muff-bag 1868

Compact and Coin Purse 1890-1910

Reticule c.1850-65

Vanity Case 1920-25

Safety Under-skirt Bag
1907

Long Purse 1860s

Chain Purse 1880s

Butterfly Brooch and Flower Holder 1868

Dress Clip 1930

Gilt Filigree and Enamel Brooch 1860-70

Dragonfly Brooch c.1900

Lizard Brooch 1932

'Mouse' Bracelet 1880

Lucky Elephant-hair and Gold Bracelet 1925-26

Gold and Hair Ring c.1870

other firms, and with transfer prints on light wood.

In the twentieth century, the etiquette of cards continued up to World War 2 and beyond, though in a diminished form. Cards were by then used mainly as a means of identification in the business world.

For those who knew each other well enough, and who were paying a visit which was to last long enough to warrant taking off one's bonnet (which a 'morning call' did not), there was one other piece of equipment which should not be passed over—the cap basket. It was perhaps already a little old fashioned when our period started, but there were still ladies, albeit elderly, who would blench at the thought of appearing with uncovered heads. For such a visit, a muslin or lace cap would be carried in a special small basket, to be donned instead of the bonnet on arrival at a friend's house. Even so, though 'visits of friendship need not be so ceremonious as those of ceremony . . . it is requisite to call at suitable times, and to avoid staying too long. . . . The courtesies of society should be ever maintained (and) serious discussions or arguments are to be altogether avoided.'

Muffs

The skin-tight fitting kid gloves worn by well-dressed women, which had to be worked on to the hands finger by finger, must have led to what the painter G. F. Watts described as 'hands squeezed into gloves too small for them . . . incapable of clasping the hand of another with the full fervour of friendship' and also to very cold fingers, liable to chilblains. The comfort of a muff would alleviate this (though not improve its capacity for friendly hand clasps). In very cold weather a small hot water bottle could be carried inside the muff, several types being available: round Doulton pottery bottles, metal ones and miniature rubber bottles. Muffs were usually of fur, smallish barrel-shaped ones in the middle of the nineteenth century and large flat ones at the end.

A muff chain was useful as it kept the muff suspended from the neck when the hands had to be free, for instance, to take money from one's purse, or for lifting the skirt out of the dirt. These chains were often linked chains of beads. A child's muff would almost always have a chain or ribbon loop to prevent its being carelessly dropped and mislaid.

Many muffs had a pocket inside that would hold a hot water bottle, a handkerchief or a purse. More usefully, they sometimes combined a bag. In 1868, Asser and Sherwin were selling Muffbags which were available in numerous different furs: black fur seal, gold fur seal, imitation seal, astrakhan or Siberian fox. The bag part of it had an ormolu frame with a double-action lock, and they cost from 25s. to 3 guineas.

In the '70s to '80s there was a fashion for both men and women to wear small wrist muffs, known as muffatees, but it never became the fashion for men to use real muffs as they did in the eighteenth century. Very large muffs (with matching enormous fur stoles) were an Edwardian fashion. Never totally out of favour, the muff made a brief return to fashion in 1930, usually made of velvet, or of a flattish fur such as breitschwantz or astrakhan. Artificial persian lamb was cheap and easy to make up at home for those who could not afford the real thing.

Handbags and Purses

The problem of carrying about one's personal impedimenta, such as purse, handkerchief, fan and so on, can be solved in two ways: by a sufficiency of pockets, or by carrying a bag of some kind and, while men in the nineteenth and twentieth centuries used the first method, women did so only for a short period in the middle of the nineteenth century—and then not entirely whole-heartedly. Since then they have opted almost unanimously for the second method. During the Regency period, when skirts hung straight to the ground, reticules had to be carried because any bulging pocket would have spoiled the hang of the skirt, and they became fashionable accessories. When skirts

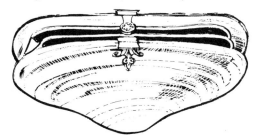

Purse made of bivalve shell. These were sold as seaside souvenirs. This one c. 1880.

widened out again, a pocket was worn, either a separate pocket under the skirt or one set into the skirt. It seems that this was eventually found insufficient, even though all that might be carried was a purse, a handkerchief and perhaps a card case. Reticules are hardly ever shown in fashion plates of the 1840s to 1860s' period, so that they were obviously not high fashion, but they were an article that was too useful to be discarded altogether; and in 1868, Messrs Simpson of Regent Street, London, had in stock not only ladies' handbags (which may have been hand luggage) and dressing bags, but also reticules in white leather. From about this time on there was an increasing demand and, in 1870, a correspondent of the *Englishwoman's Domestic Magazine* wrote of 'the leather bags known as Cabas, now to be seen in every lady's hand'. These may have been made of strips of leather 'woven in imitation of wickerwork' which was a fashionable craze for a time (Fr. *cabas* = basket). A dark blue or black velvet bag with polished steel beads was fashionable in the '60s and later into the twentieth century, although the beads were more usually replaced by a silver mount and initials. Sometimes these bags or reticules hung from the belt and might be partnered by a matching Dagger fan. By 1888, handbags in the modern sense were being used; in December of that year Mappin and Webb issued an illustrated advertisement showing a Lady's Calf Handbag with oxidised mounts at 7s. 6d., which would not look amiss today. By the early

[53]

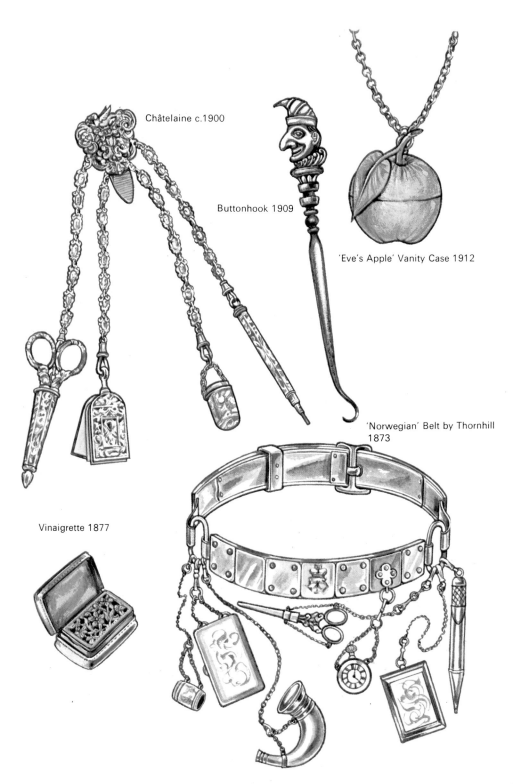

Châtelaine c.1900

Buttonhook 1909

'Eve's Apple' Vanity Case 1912

'Norwegian' Belt by Thornhill 1873

Vinaigrette 1877

[54]

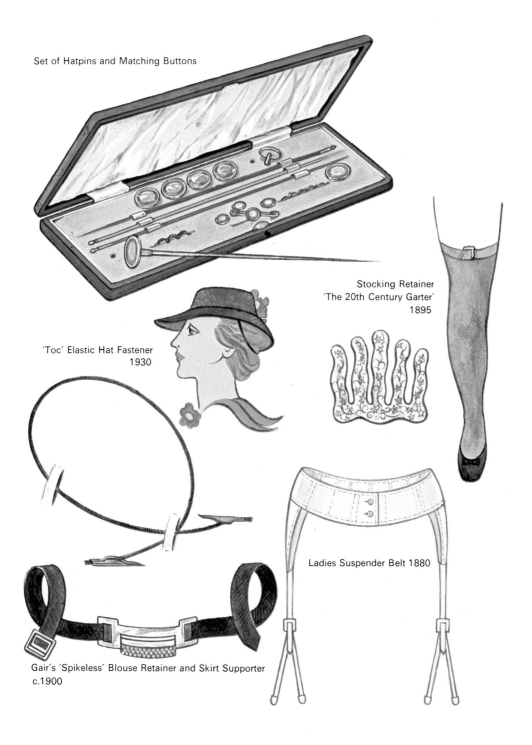

Set of Hatpins and Matching Buttons

Stocking Retainer
'The 20th Century Garter'
1895

'Toc' Elastic Hat Fastener
1930

Ladies Suspender Belt 1880

Gair's 'Spikeless' Blouse Retainer and Skirt Supporter
c.1900

twentieth century leather bags were variously fitted out as Vanity Bags when fitted with pockets containing powder and puff, scent bottle and mirror, or as Purse Bags with a built-in purse. Special bags for special occasions included an Opera Bag by the Alexander Clarke Manufacturing Co., in fine quality suede or crocodile, containing opera glasses, fan, mirror, and powder-puff, all for £3. 7s. 6d. (1905). For travelling, many women reverted to the old-fashioned idea of a pocket under the skirt—in this case one divided into separate compartments for money, tickets and other valuables. A money-belt might be worn by men, or at least a bag that was firmly strapped to the body and hence less likely to be either lost or stolen.

A popular purse right through until the last quarter of the nineteenth century was the long purse (also known as a miser's or stocking purse). This was used back in the eighteenth century and there were still instructions for making them in the needlework pages of magazines in the 1870s. Knitted, netted or crocheted in silk or cotton, with or without beads, part of their popularity was probably that they could be made at home. Money was inserted through a central slit, pushed down to one end, and kept in its place by sliding down one of the two metal rings to close off the end. A more utilitarian form of this purse was made of chamois leather; they were used by both sexes. Sovereign cases were small

Silver sovereign case, to take five sovereigns, with ring to hang from watch chain

round cases resembling watch cases, usually of engine-turned silver, and made to take sovereigns (£1 in gold), the coins being held in position by a spring; similar oval cases held sovereigns and half-sovereigns. A larger, oblong purse had spaces for half-crowns, shillings and sixpences, and a pocket for bank notes or cards as well, and one was part vanity case.

Metal mesh bags and purses were used at the end of the century; and in gold or silver, as evening bags until well into the 1920s. Before the twentieth century, evening bags or reticules were seldom used—what with wielding fans, bouquets and dance programmes it would have been difficult. Though make-up was, if not the rule, at least a very frequent exception, it was certainly not done to repair one's face anywhere but in the privacy of a bedroom, and there was therefore little need of a case to carry powder and lip rouge. But as soon as making-up was no longer supposed to be secret, and running repairs were considered necessary during the course of an evening, then, of course, a suitable container became a matter of importance—sometimes it took the form of a petit point, beaded, or painted silk bag (which might also contain a small matching

[56]

fan); or a vanity case, such as Eve's Apple, sold by Hunt and Roskill Ltd, Old Bond Street, London, in 1912. A black composition and diamanté case of the 1920s, when open, disclosed powder and rouge and compartments for cigarettes and matches—a hanging tassel concealed a lipstick.

Châtelaines

Yet a third, though considerably less convenient, method of carrying about small belongings, was by means of a châtelaine hooked to the belt; sewing equipment, such as small scissors in a case, a pin cushion and thimble case, with writing tablets (usually thin slices of ivory) and a pencil, formed the usual complement, all hanging from chains. Other items, such as a small scent bottle

Glasses-case in chased silver with 1894 date-letter and with châtelaine hook to hang from belt

or a spectacle case might be added. In the nineteenth century, châtelaines were as a rule worn only in the house, though in the eighteenth they are sometimes depicted out-of-doors. Cut steel was a favourite, then and in the 1850s and '60s, but when they came back into fashion in the early '70s, silver, or the next best thing, electroplate, was preferred—by this time, though no doubt worn sometimes for convenience, they were considered more as a fashionable ornament than a useful accessory, being described as 'more fashionable than a watch chain'. Designs were also different. They no longer depended on the sparkle of steel facets, but took on a post-mediaeval look, with grotesque faces on the supporting top, or, sometimes, a classical air.

A different form can never have been more than an occasional oddity—one of Messrs Thornhill's famous novelties, the Norwegian Belt, in 1873, was of leather with metal plaques and was hung around with every conceivable gadget.

Lorgnettes and Reading Glasses

The idea of a lorgnette nowadays brings to mind a rather haughty lady condescending to something really rather beneath her notice, probably because it was fashionable at the time when the Edwardian figure was at its most imposing. The lorgnette was, in a way, the successor to the single eye-glass of the earlier nineteenth century, which was much used, rudely one might think, for

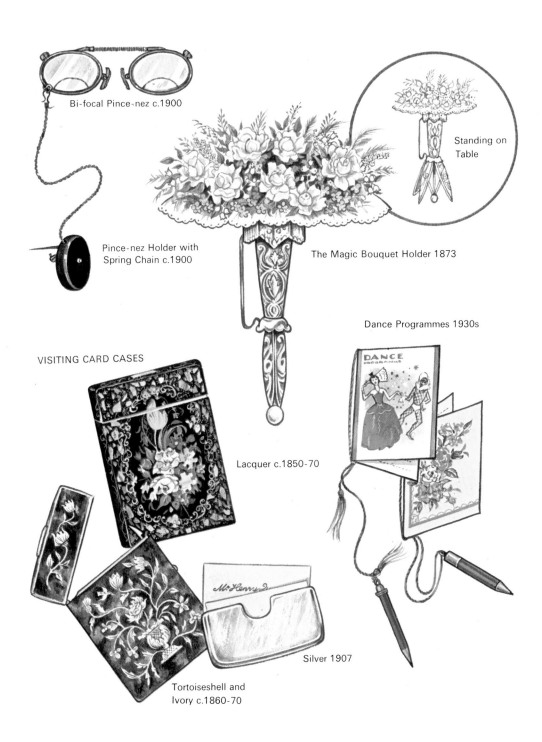

Bi-focal Pince-nez c.1900

Standing on Table

Pince-nez Holder with Spring Chain c.1900

The Magic Bouquet Holder 1873

Dance Programmes 1930s

VISITING CARD CASES

DANCE PROGRAMME

Lacquer c.1850-70

Mr Henry D

Silver 1907

Tortoiseshell and Ivory c.1860-70

Red Feather Fan 1880s

Empire Style Fan c.1890

Black Net Fan with
Steel Sequins
1860s

Souvenir Fan from
Hotel Martinique, New York,
'Dutch Room', early 1900s

Dagger Fan, Sheath with
'Châtelaine' Hook
1870s

[59]

'quizzing' people. By the middle of the century there were numerous 'hand double-eyeglasses', folding and non-folding, which were no doubt precursors of the lorgnette with the long handle. It was, in fact, very useful for those who did not need to wear glasses all the time, or who refused to do so. The spectacles of the time were mostly exceedingly unbecoming, with very small oval lenses, and the attempt to make them less so resulted in the so-called 'invisible' glasses, or pince-nez, which left dents in the sides of the nose and were, in addition, very liable to fall off. Hence they were usually anchored to the dress or coat by some kind of chain or cord. The holder illustrated, with a retractable chain on a spring, meant that they could be worn only when needed and carried in a conveniently accessible position.

Glasses in lacquered wooden case, lined velvet c. 1880

The lorgnette illustrated on page 63 had, however, another function—it was a discreet deaf-aid. Made of tortoiseshell, it was supplied by Frank-Valéry, Boulevard des Capucins, Paris:

> 'The most elegant, the most discreet Auditory apparatus, it is above all the proper apparatus for the use of ladies whose hearing is affected, and its power is such that they can hear at the theatre, in church and even in a parlour, as though they were endowed with the finest hearing.'

The price of this Auditory Lorgnette was 56s. in 1901 (which would put it well into the luxury class) and the firm also made Auditory Walking Sticks for gentlemen.

Some Other Accessories

Accessories such as fans, châtelaines or even lorgnettes can be considered not only in terms of utility—they were also often decorative and fashionable. There is another class of personal accessory which is only useful, being inconspicuous or even unseen.

A problem that took an unduly long time to solve satisfactorily was the best way to keep up stockings. Corsets did not have suspenders attached until rather late in the Victorian period (though there are suggestions of tapes, loops and buttons), so that most women wore garters, which constricted the legs and caused varicose veins. In 1880 L. Hoven claimed that the Improved Patent

Stocking Suspender had entirely superseded garters. This suspender was a belt resembling a modern suspender belt and, according to the advertisements, had the following advantages:

'1. It allows free circulation of the blood.
2. It leaves no mark on the limbs.
3. It holds the stocking firmly and without a wrinkle.
4. It cannot tear the stocking under any circumstance.'

Prices were, for ladies, 2s. 6d. in cotton or 4s. in silk. There were also models for 'young Ladies' and for children, and sock suspenders for gentlemen.

This was not the only one. Very soon after, there was also the New Stocking Suspender (Cramp's patent), sold by T. Jenkin of Newgate Street, London, and another, in 1891, was made by the Warren Hose Supporter Company: 'the Warren is absolutely perfect'. But for all that, women appear to have clung to their garters, however uncomfortable and unhealthy, and in 1895 the Duchess Stocking Retainer made its appearance. It called itself 'the Twentieth Century Garter' and was expected to replace all other 'garters, suspenders, etc' and hold stockings without a wrinkle. It is not at all clear that this invention could ever have been more successful than the old emergency device of twisting a coin in the stocking welt.

Most of the forward-tilted hats in the 1930s were fitted with their own elastic to hold them in place, but for those which were not there was the Elastic Hat Fastener. This was not the first hat-holding device, though apart from pins it was probably the first which aimed at keeping the hat actually on the head—a cord with a clip at each end had been in use earlier and was used by men particularly, to keep straw boaters from flying away. In this case one end of the cord was fastened to the coat lapel.

The Gair Blouse Spikeless Retainer and Skirt Supporter was especially a boon when blouses and skirts were fashionable during the late nineteenth and early twentieth century, when blouses were constantly trying to escape from the waistband. Another grip, in 1895, was the Leopold Skirt Grip which was 'the most successful novelty of the year'. It prevented the skirt dropping away from the waist at the back where the fastening usually was.

Patent hatguard, on original card 1910–20

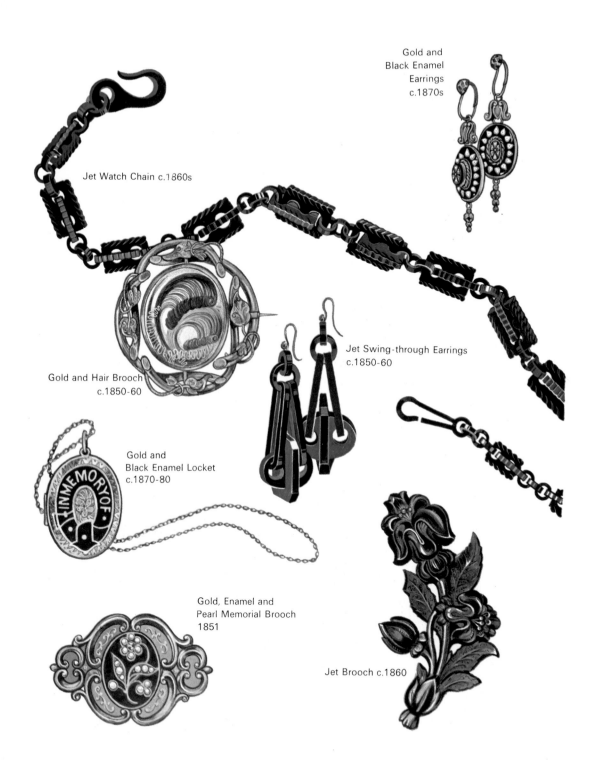

Gold and
Black Enamel
Earrings
c.1870s

Jet Watch Chain c.1860s

Gold and Hair Brooch
c.1850-60

Jet Swing-through Earrings
c.1850-60

Gold and
Black Enamel Locket
c.1870-80

Gold, Enamel and
Pearl Memorial Brooch
1851

Jet Brooch c.1860

IN MEMORY OF

Tortoiseshell, Jet and
Tortoiseshell with Piqué Combs

Tie Pins,
2nd half of
19th century

1860s

c.1870

c.1900

Cuff Links 1920s

Shirt Studs and Links
c.1870-90s

Crocodile Opera Bag 1905

Tortoiseshell
'Auditory' Lorgnette 1901

Tortoiseshell
Magnifying Glass,
2nd half of 19th century

4
SEWING
AND WRITING

Sewing

It was not until the middle of the nineteenth century that Sewing Machines suitable for domestic use were available to lighten the labours of women sewing either for their families or for a precarious living. Although the earliest patent was taken out by an Englishman, Thomas Saint, in 1799, most of the popular domestic machines came from the USA. Almost the first, and certainly one of the most popular, was the Singer Family Machine (1858), followed by the New Family Machine in 1865; these were lockstitch machines. The purchaser in the nineteenth century had the choice of three types of stitch—lockstitch, chain-stitch and two-thread chain-stitch. Ordinary chain-stitch had the disadvantage of easily coming undone if the thread was not fastened off properly, or if the thread broke, and users of these machines were advised to go over their seams twice to guard against this. However, these machines were extremely popular, as is proved by the numbers still surviving, especially Willcox and Gibbs machines. Willcox and Gibbs manufactured both hand and treadle machines, and also a small machine which could be detached from the treadle stand and instantly converted to hand use. James Weir, too, produced a small, light-weight, inexpensive hand machine. This also used a chain-stitch and was small enough to use on practically any table. It was quite usual for a family to have two machines, one of these a lightweight machine that could be used even in the sitting-room, and a treadle machine for heavy work.

Many old sewing machines are elaborately decorated with gilded and inlaid mother-of-pearl ornament. That they were tough as well as ornamental and useful is proved by the large numbers that still survive in good working order.

Probably the smallest-ever machine was the Moldacott Pocket Machine, invented by a German, Rosenthal, and manufactured in London in 1887. This was clamped to the edge of a table when in use and fitted into a small case which could be carried in any reasonably large pocket. The Albion Combination Machine, reported in *The Queen* in 1875, was said to make 'four distinct kinds of sewing, viz. Lock stitch, Chain-stitch, Lock Chain-stitch and Combination or Changeable sewing—four machines in one, at the price of any other first class machine which only makes one stitch'. The price of this marvel was £4. 4s., about the same as the Singer Family Machine.

In the 1860s and '70s there was much correspondence in magazines and newspapers concerning sewing machines, their respective merits and disadvantages. In *The Queen* of 3 October 1863, one reader strongly recommended Newton, Wilson and Co.'s machines, while another, who had plainly made a thorough survey of the machines available, recommended Willcox and Gibbs for chain-stitch, Singer, and Wheeler and Wilson for lockstitch, and Newton, Wilson and Co.'s machines for 'double loop stitch' (two-thread chain-stitch) and embroidery.

By the 1870s few households were without a machine of some kind. Isaac Singer, and some other firms, made it easier for the impoverished purchaser, who could not afford to pay the money down, by instituting the instalment system.

One result of the lightening of labour by this machine, was an increase in the amount of trimming put on to dresses. Once the principle of the sewing machine had been established, it was a comparatively easy matter to design improvements and attachments—Wheeler and Wilson's Prize Medal Machine in 1863 already had attachments for binding, cording, gathering and pleating.

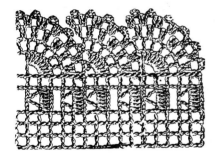

Purled lace edging: directions in the Girls' Own Annual *1884*

Embroidery of a simple kind could be executed with some of these machines, but a small hand tool was also available from 1897. It was first introduced in the *World of Fashion* as La Fée du Foyer 'for the rapid execution of beautifully modelled and coloured designs... highly raised in silk, or wool, on any material, from leather to muslin'. It produced 'a maximum of decorative effect, by a minimum of very interesting work requiring no artistic knowledge'. What appears to be a very similar machine was patented in 1918 and another, advertised in Weldon's Bazaar in 1925, called the Ideal, 'enables even a child to embroider with remarkable beauty in wool or silk on any material'. A more utilitarian gadget was the Star Darner—for darning made easy, in stockings,

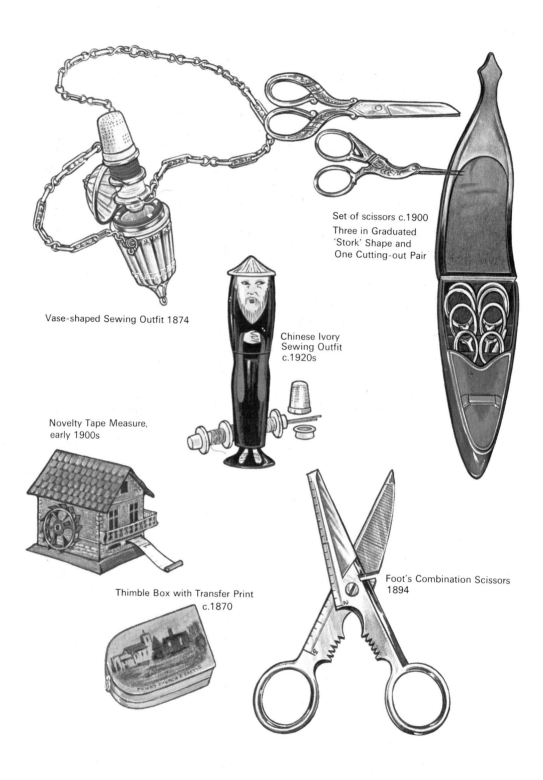

Vase-shaped Sewing Outfit 1874

Set of scissors c.1900
Three in Graduated
'Stork' Shape and
One Cutting-out Pair

Chinese Ivory
Sewing Outfit
c.1920s

Novelty Tape Measure,
early 1900s

Thimble Box with Transfer Print
c.1870

Foot's Combination Scissors
1894

[66]

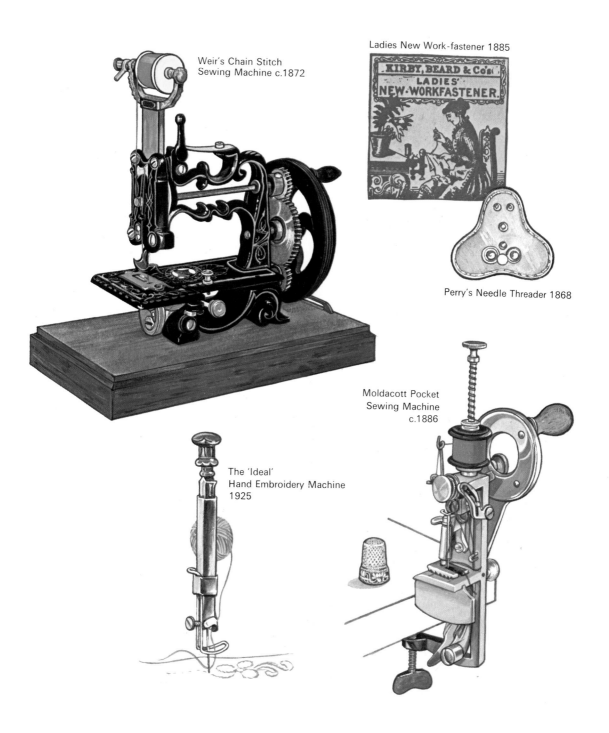

Weir's Chain Stitch
Sewing Machine c.1872

Ladies New Work-fastener 1885

Perry's Needle Threader 1868

The 'Ideal'
Hand Embroidery Machine
1925

Moldacott Pocket
Sewing Machine
c.1886

[67]

Wooden glove-darning stick, the small end for fingers and the larger for thumbs, mid 19th century

table linen and so on. It enabled a neater darn to be woven by lifting alternate threads, as do the heddles on a loom. The Spedi-weve in the late 1930s did the same thing.

In spite of the wide and rapid spread of the domestic sewing machine in the nineteenth century, it was mainly used for dress-making and larger items of household linen. For smaller or more delicate pieces, the tradition of hand needlework was still maintained and most women who had any leisure at all had not altogether lost their skills or their appreciation of fine workmanship. Machine-made articles would be finished by hand and others, such as christening gowns and other baby clothes, were often made by hand. Elaborate lingerie for a trousseau might also be hand-made and in fact, right up to the 1920s and '30s, the more expensive underwear, even bought ready-made, was often finished by hand. Much exquisitely fine work was still produced in convents. So the ability to 'sew a fine seam' was by no means a dead letter and books on needlecraft, such as Thérèse de Dillmont's *Encyclopedia of Needlework* in 1880, were bestsellers—the *Encyclopedia* gave detailed instructions on almost every conceivable kind of needlework, from tatting to canvas stitches.

Magazines also issued patterns, for dresses and other garments and also for embroidery: for Madeira work (broderie anglaise), white work, silk embroidery and, above all, for the ever-popular Berlin woolwork, which was used for working chair seats and backs, slippers, teacosies, footstools, braces and even waistcoats, with or without added beadwork, not to mention copies of paintings—those by Landseer being particular favourites. This work had been popular since the early nineteenth century—it was comparatively easy, covered the ground fast, and was not such a strain on the eyes as, for instance, fine whitework. The coloured patterns on squared paper, first produced on a large scale by Wittich's of Berlin, meant that a beginner could hardly go wrong and, above all, there was an end product that was usually extremely showy and sometimes useful. No one could ignore, though one might not admire, chairs worked in brilliant floral designs, sometimes even with flowers in relief in 'plush-stitch'. However, while it was interesting and absorbing to work the design, tedium often set in with the working of plain grounds, hence, no doubt, many unfinished articles and also such offers as this, in the *Englishwoman's Domestic Magazine* of February 1871:

'1093. STEPHANIE grounds Berlin wool work at moderate prices. Address with Editor.'

[68]

Pattern for dressing table mats, from the Girls' Own Annual *1884*

Whitework was the very antithesis of woolwork, in colour, effect, and the degree of skill required. A good deal was therefore commissioned work, executed by professional embroideresses, but there were still many who embroidered their own handkerchiefs, *engageantes* (1850s to '60s) or under-sleeves, and baby clothes. Broderie Anglaise was one most popular form of this—patterns being formed by a series of holes with overcast edges. For this work a Stiletto was an essential tool. Tatting, which is more nearly allied to lace-making, as it involves no background material, was another craft popular-ised by Thérèse de Dillmont. This was worked in a series of knots with a tatting shuttle of bone, mother-of-pearl or ivory, and a pin known as a purling pin; worked rings were joined together to form lace-like trimmings, doileys or dressing table mats. Netting, knitting and crochet were all used for the making of silk purses sometimes with steel beads (see Chapter 3, *Accessories*) and other articles. Netting needles of bone or steel, with gauges usually of bone or wood, sometimes shared a case with stilettos, tambour hooks and other tools. The tambour hook, resembling a very fine crochet hook, was used for chain-stitch embroidery and, to protect its fine tip, often the hook could be pulled out of the handle and reversed into it, thus forming a case. The name Tambour came from the fact that this work was originally done on a drum-shaped frame tambour = drum).

The fundamental tool for sewing is the needle. Long before 1850 fine steel needles were on the market, adapted in shape and size to the many different

[69]

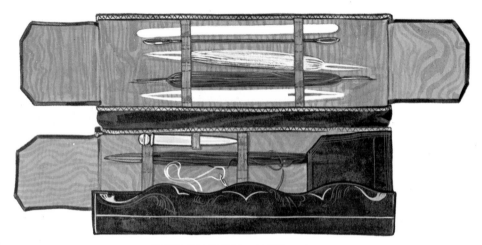

Netting Needle Case, mid 19th century

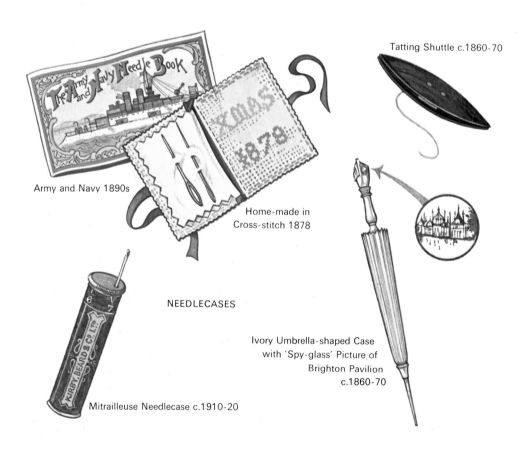

Tatting Shuttle c.1860-70

The Army and Navy Needle Book

XMAS 1878

Army and Navy 1890s

Home-made in
Cross-stitch 1878

NEEDLECASES

Ivory Umbrella-shaped Case
with 'Spy-glass' Picture of
Brighton Pavilion
c.1860-70

Mitrailleuse Needlecase c.1910-20

[70]

Pincushion Love-token c.1880

Standard Pin Box,
early 20th century

Cotton-reel Stand 1880s

Hannum Pinking Machine 1897

[71]

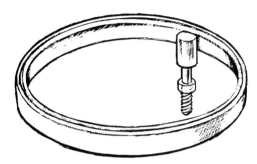

*Embroidery frame with table clamp
1920–30*

kinds of sewing and embroidery then popular: fine small needles for whitework, crewel needles for wool embroidery, tapestry needles for Berlin woolwork on canvas, etc. Very fine needles created problems for those with poor sight or inadequate spectacles, for which various solutions were suggested. In 1873, egg-eyed needles were advertised by Millikin and Lawley, The Strand, London, 'rendering the eye miraculously distinct for threading'. They are 'a boon to all who from failing sight, or nervous trembling of the hand are unable to thread the eye of an ordinary needle'. Two hundred of these excellent needles in assorted sizes cost 2s. 6d.! The calyx-eyed needle which had a split at the eye into which the thread could be sprung was another suggestion and there was also Perry and Co.'s Patent Needle Threader, which 'instrument will be appreciated for its simplicity and the smallness of its cost. It enables a person almost blind to thread a needle equally well as those having the perfect use of their sight.' These were 1s. each in 1868. Probably these aids were of most use to women who did hand-sewing for a living and whose eyesight was failing in consequence.

An embroidery needle with the eye in the centre and a point at each end was patented by Hayes and Crossley in 1866. This was alleged to make work faster and easier by making it unnecessary to turn the needle when making the next stitch. The 'tapering needles of Messrs Hayes & Crossley', alluded to by 'Silkworm' of the *Englishwoman's Domestic Magazine* in June 1871 may be this same invention. They 'are wonderfully easy to work with, for, being tapered at both ends, they offer half the resistance of ordinary needles to the fabric, and are invaluable for sewing on silk and on muslin'.

Although needles were sold in paper packets they were often transferred to special needle cases, or to needle books which might be home-made. Tubular ivory needle cases were sometimes part of the fittings of a workbox, and cases carved in the shape of a closed umbrella could be bought as souvenirs in most holiday resorts (doubtless to remind the visitor of the state of the weather!). These had a small peep-hole in the handle, showing minute views of the locality through a magnifying lens. One such shows no fewer than six views of Bournemouth through a hole 3 mm in diameter, and came from Beale's Store—the one illustrated on page 70 was a souvenir from Brighton.

[72]

Needle books had inner pages of flannel with pinked edges and covers of various materials, punched card with decorative stitching being used for home-made ones—often with a greeting and date embroidered on them. Later needle cases were manufactured of metal or leatherette and were mostly severely practical. Some were still tube-shaped, as for instance the Mitrailleuse, c. 1907, from which a needle of the pre-selected size would be ejected. To keep needles sharp and rust-free, Victorian women used a small cushion of emery powder in and out of which the needle would be pushed—these were very often made in the shape of a strawberry, of red felt with the seeds either embroidered on or represented by yellow beads.

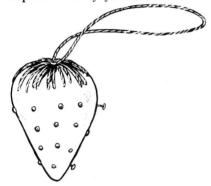

Strawberry cushion filled with emery for cleaning pins and needles, mid 19th century

Pins were another necessity. In the early nineteenth century they had been used not only in dress-making, but also to fasten dresses; and they continued to be used to fix on trimmings for much longer. A pincushion was therefore necessary for the dressing-room, in addition to that used for sewing. Pins were bought in 'papers', that is rows of pins stuck into a folded sheet of paper, sometimes of mixed sizes: 'A paper of mixed pins' (*David Copperfield*: Charles Dickens); and it was still possible to buy pins this way (and needles too) quite recently. Small packets of pins were offered by many haberdashers, at any rate up to the 1940s, in lieu of a farthing change. There were large, practical pincushions, usually stuffed with sawdust, but also very many, meant to be carried in the pocket or reticule, that seem to have been designed to hold as few pins as possible. Many of these, again, were sold as souvenirs and from these, perhaps, the buyer did not expect too much in the way of utility. A very much flattened cushion of velvet, sandwiched between two discs of polished wood embellished with transfer prints of local beauty spots, offered only a narrow ring of velvet in which to stick the pins. At seaside places, small bivalve shells had cushions stuffed into them and were sold as pincushions. Yet another kind of pincushion was made, traditionally as a love token by sailors at sea in their off-duty hours, to present to their sweethearts when they came ashore. These cushions were usually very large, heart-shaped, and decorated with designs stuck out in pins with large coloured heads. Anchors were naturally a favourite motif, as a reminder of the donor's occupation or as a symbol of hope.

[73]

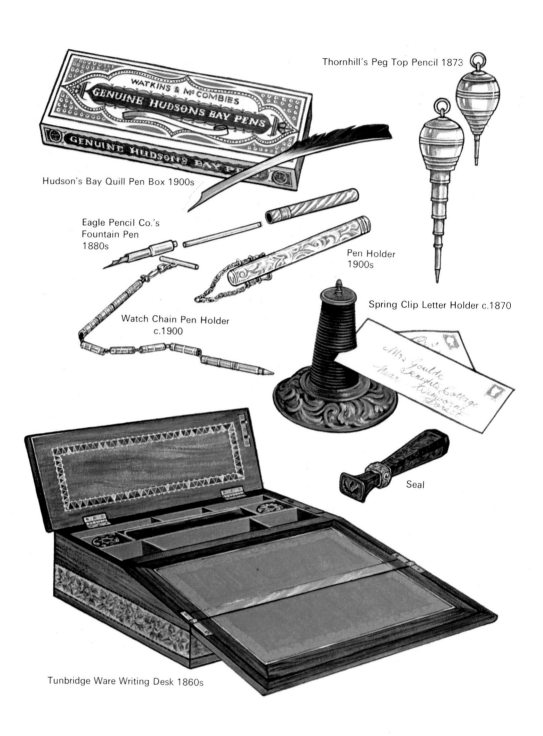

Hudson's Bay Quill Pen Box 1900s

Thornhill's Peg Top Pencil 1873

Eagle Pencil Co.'s
Fountain Pen
1880s

Pen Holder
1900s

Watch Chain Pen Holder
c.1900

Spring Clip Letter Holder c.1870

Seal

Tunbridge Ware Writing Desk 1860s

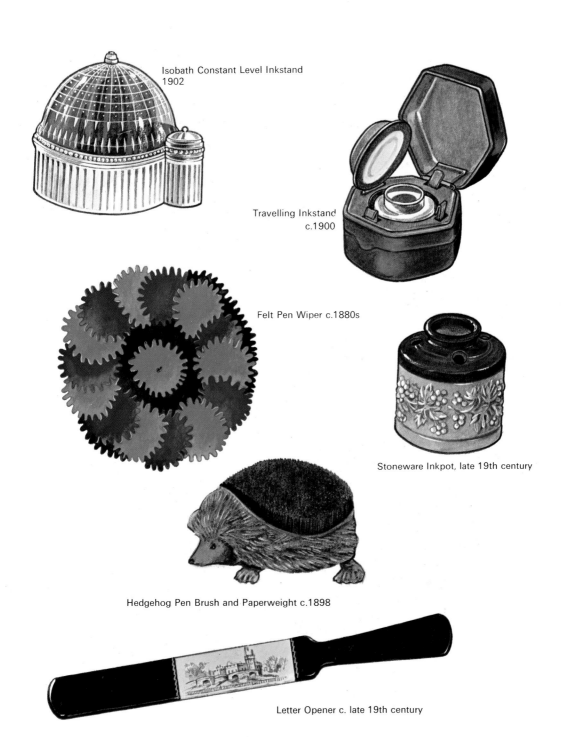

Isobath Constant Level Inkstand
1902

Travelling Inkstand
c.1900

Felt Pen Wiper c.1880s

Stoneware Inkpot, late 19th century

Hedgehog Pen Brush and Paperweight c.1898

Letter Opener c. late 19th century

By the 1850s the method of winding cottons and silks on to wooden reels was in use and there was no longer the need to wind off skeins at home, except for special embroidery silks. Work boxes from this time therefore contain spaces for reels, or spindles on to which they could be slipped, instead of the earlier mother-of-pearl or bone winders and reels. Another method of keeping a large number of reels was the Reel Stand, of wood or heavy brass. These were made to revolve so that the wanted colour could easily be turned to the front, and the reel revolved on its spindle as the thread was pulled off. Necessarily, in that time of busy needlewomen, cotton and silk sewing thread was made in a great many more varieties, thicknesses and colours than nowadays, when it is sometimes impossible to get sewing thread any finer than the 60 grade. This is clear from the table of cottons available from D.M.C., in Thérèse de Dillmont's *Encyclopedia*: plain sewing or machine cotton could then be had in twenty-four different grades, from twenty to seven hundred, and in four hundred and fifty colours plus black and white.

Sewing clamps were commonly used in the eighteenth and nineteenth centuries; they held one end of the work firm so that the seamstress could keep the work taut with one hand while stitching with the other. When all work had to be done by hand, this speeded up long seams or hems considerably and kept stitching even; but the introduction of the sewing machine made most of these clamps redundant. There must, however, still have been a demand, for in 1885 Messrs Kirby, Beard brought out a Ladies' New Work Fastener, which was advertised in *The Queen*. Though rather more elaborate, this clamp had all the features of the older ones, including the pin cushion on the top.

Scissors could of course be bought singly, but where much dress-making or needlework was done it was preferable to have a choice. In addition to large cutting-out shears, several sizes could be bought in a set having their own satin-lined leather case (1907). A pair of buttonhole scissors was a useful tool, besides. The ultimate in combination tools must have been the scissors advertised in 1880 by J. Wilder (though some pocket knives ran them close). These scissors claimed to be: buttonhole scissors, cigar-cutter, gas pliers, nail scissors, nail file, wire cutter, screwdriver, ink eraser [?], paperknife, pen-nib extractor and three-inch measure. In an advertisement of 1894 they manage, in addition, to be a coin tester and railway carriage key.

Frills and flounces often had 'pinked' edges, that is, they were cut out in fancy toothed designs, both as a means of decoration and to prevent fraying out. Even in the 1850s and '60s, when flounces were much in evidence, these edges were laboriously achieved by means of a punch, a block of lead, and a mallet, the punches being available in many designs. Hannum's Pinking Machine, patented in 1897, put an end to all that: it was clamped to a table and by turning the handle, yard upon yard of pinked borders could be turned out comparatively effortlessly. Pinking shears, which produced a plain toothed edge mainly used to trim internal seams, were a later invention.

Small folding case for tatting, containing shuttle, purling pin and scissors c. 1870

The nineteenth-century mania for gadgets produced a fine crop of miniature sewing outfits or hussifs. Such was an ivory egg (rather before our period) which unscrewed to divulge a central needlecase acting as a spindle for a diminutive double reel for thread, a metal finger guard and an ivory thimble; so beautifully made is this egg that the dividing line is invisible even under magnification. Another container, of silver, was made to hang from a châtelaine or belt; it was urn-shaped and held a ring pincushion of purple velvet, with needles, thread and thimble in the centre. Small compendia disguised as books with tooled leather covers contained ivory writing tablets and a small pencil as well as sewing equipment. But the most portable of all was the Running Repair Brooch, which contained needles and thread in its bar, for emergency repairs.

Writing

Nowadays, when nearly everyone has access to a telephone, this is the most frequent and convenient mode of social (and business) communication. It was different in the nineteenth century—a note or letter was necessary to pass on even the most trivial message unless it could be done by word of mouth. This meant that letters were of far greater importance in family and social life than they are today. Writing good letters, then and in earlier generations, was an art which was cultivated deliberately in many families from childhood on. To look back to the letters of Fanny Burney in the eighteenth century and of Mrs Gaskell in the nineteenth, and all the other collections of letters—not to mention the novels written in letter form such as *Evelina* and *Clarissa*—makes one realise that this was a highly regarded accomplishment. It seems at that time to have been particularly developed in women, perhaps because their intellectual capacities at that time were so seldom able to develop in other directions. Letter-writing was, therefore, to some an outlet and to nearly all a necessity in some degree, in order to keep in touch with friends and relatives living outside

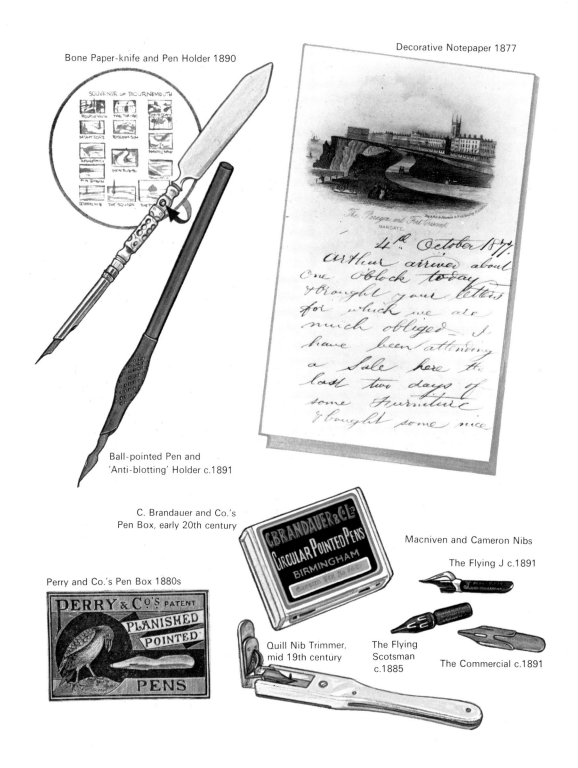

Bone Paper-knife and Pen Holder 1890

Decorative Notepaper 1877

Ball-pointed Pen and 'Anti-blotting' Holder c.1891

C. Brandauer and Co.'s Pen Box, early 20th century

Macniven and Cameron Nibs

The Flying J c.1891

Perry and Co.'s Pen Box 1880s

Quill Nib Trimmer, mid 19th century

The Flying Scotsman c.1885

The Commercial c.1891

Black Lacquered Wood Pencil Box c.1880s

Wooden Roll-ruler and
Pencil Box c.1890

Caw's Safety
Fountain Pen 1898

Swan Ink Dropper 1900

Goodall's Mourning Notepaper 1891

Pelican Self-feeding Pen 1896

'Ideal' Safety Pen
by Waterman 1883

Onoto Lever-filling
Fountain Pen 1925-26

easy visiting distance—visiting was of course much more restricted at a time when there were no cars and little public transport. Greater formality than obtains nowadays, in the conduct of life at least of the middle and upper classes, meant many letters—of invitation, congratulation, thanks—where now a word will do, then a formal letter was thought necessary.

Penny postage, the brainchild of Rowland Hill, had been introduced in 1840 and was the means of greatly reducing the cost of sending a letter, thus bringing it within the scope of a far larger number of people, far more often, than before. The old habit of 'crossing' the paper, in order to save the expense of sending a second sheet, became rarer and letters more legible, though it was still done on occasions well past the middle of the century.

Nearly all regular writers had their own writing desk; not a writing table, but a portable box which opened out to form a convenient slope for writing on; the correct angle was held to be most important in the development of good handwriting. These desks (also called writing slopes) had compartments for writing paper, ink bottles, pens and all the necessary equipment, and were veneered or leather covered—the one illustrated on page 74 is of Tunbridge Ware (a form of marquetry) of the 1860s. They could be carried from room to room and were taken on journeys.

Quills were for centuries the usual writing instrument, the feathers most in demand being the wing feathers of geese and swans. Quills were not seriously rivalled by metal nibs until the middle of the century and, even after this, quills and quill nibs continued to be used for many purposes. Quill nibs, which were cut from a quill and used in a penholder, were the invention of Thomas Palmer of East Grinstead, who subsequently held the Royal Warrant as penmaker to George III, and in the early nineteenth century Joseph Bramah (who invented the Bramah lock) perfected a machine for cutting several nibs out of one quill. The first metal nibs were made in the eighteenth century, but for a long time they were unsatisfactory in that they were much harder and less flexible than a quill; and though steel nibs had the advantage of not having to be re-trimmed at frequent intervals, yet this advantage was not always a merit, as a quill could be 'mended' to suit the writer:

'The young lady . . . went accidentally into the school room to get a pen mended. . . . "Shall it be a hard or a soft nib?" inquired Nicholas' (*Nicholas Nickleby:* Charles Dickens).

Nibs were trimmed to shape with a pen-knife, originally used for this purpose alone, though it came to mean almost any small folding pocket knife. A special quill cutter, incorporating a knife and a clipping tool, was also used.

Messrs Macniven and Cameron were penmakers in Edinburgh since 1770 and were later the inventors of three famous nibs which were celebrated (and advertised) in the following rhyme:

'They come as a boon and a blessing to men,
The Pickwick, the Owl, and the Waverley Pen.'

Much effort went into improving the smoothness of metal nibs. Perry's, who had been one of the earliest manufacturers of metal nibs, in the 1880s produced a 'planished Point' nib; Ormiston and Glass (also of Edinburgh) in 1884 were selling Hewitt's Patent Ball-pointed pens 'as used by the Prince of Wales'—these were nibs with a ball-shaped point, not a modern ball-point—and in 1885 Brandauer's Circular-pointed pens also were an attempt to give flexibility and a smooth glide over the paper combined with an easy flow of ink. These were still used in the 1930s.

Writing with a quill or steel pen, not to mention some of the leaky early fountain pens, made it essential to have some simple means of removing surplus ink and to clean the nib after use. Simple penwipers were made of black felt, cut into various shapes and stitched together, this kind often being made at home. More elaborate ones could be purchased, sometimes animals or birds made of silver or other metal, with a hollow in the back filled with bristles to wipe the pen (similar mounts with velvet cushions instead of bristles served as pin cushions). An anti-blotting penholder kept the fingers clean, while unspillable ink bottles prevented calamitous stains on the furniture. De La Rue's Isobath inkstand kept the ink secure from dust and evaporation and had a float 'so weighted and poised as always to keep the ink in the dipping well at the same level'. Special safety bottles were carried when travelling: the leather-covered bottle illustrated was made in Vienna. Other necessary equipment for a bureau included an inkstand and pen tray, a blotting pad and a container for postage stamps. Sealing wax and a seal might also be necessary.

In the nineteenth century glossy white or cream paper was the general rule, though blue was also used. The paper might be die-stamped at the stationer's, but many people possessed their own embossing stamp to add the address at home. In addition to plain paper, writing paper could also be had with decorative headings, usually showing a view of the house or a local beauty spot (or, for the billheads and stationery of tradesmen, illustrations demonstrating their specialities). At holiday resorts such paper could be bought and it was provided in some hotels too, for the use of guests—a way of advertising the amenities of the place to a wider circle. Mourning paper had a more or less wide black border, according to the degree of mourning (there were rules about this) and also according to taste. Too wide a border was considered ostentatious and not in good taste. Another kind of mourning paper was produced in 1891 by Charles Goodall and Son, at a time when excessive mourning was going out of fashion. This was decorated with sprays of black foliage and other designs and was 'specially produced to meet the reviving taste for Mourning Stationery of a MORE ARTISTIC and LESS SOMBRE CHARACTER'. How this scored under the good taste rule can only be surmised.

Envelopes were not much used in England before the Penny Post was introduced, though they were more popular in France. Letters were folded with the blank side outwards and sealed with wax (black wax was used during mourning). At the Great Exhibition of 1851, Jeremiah Smith (Inventor and Manufacturer) showed gummed envelopes 'requiring neither wax nor wafer' and James Dudman exhibited three different 'self sealing' envelopes. It is not clear whether Smith's envelopes had to be licked or spread with the thumb, but Dudman's were made with a 'cement' on the flaps, protected by foil. But many still preferred the old-fashioned method of sealing wax, on which would be imprinted the writer's seal. Sticks of sealing wax, a taper or candle, and a seal would then be kept in the bureau, or the desk. Seals could be hung from the watch chain, in which case they might be merely ornamental, or a signet ring might be worn, but it was usual to have one for the desk as well. Any of these seals would have on its face the writer's identifying emblem, crest or initials, in some hard stone, such as cornelian, or in glass or metal. For notes by hand it was customary to use wafers, small gummed circles in imitation of sealing wax; but gilt or silver wafers were more frivolous:

> 'The servant brought in a very small note in a beautiful pink envelope. . . . The address of this note was written in a beautiful female hand, and the gummed wafer bore on it an impress of a gilt coronet' (*Barchester Towers:* Anthony Trollope).

By the 1880s, the steel nib pen and the quill were beginning to have rivals in the form of fountain pens. Attempts to do away with constant dipping in the inkwell had been going on for a very long time, and took two forms: firstly, adaptation of the nib to hold extra ink, as is done now with some lettering pens, and, secondly, by providing the penholder with a reservoir for ink. Both these types were originally called 'Fountain' pens but the name stuck only to the second, more important class. The pen made by the Eagle Pencil Co. of New York had a metal barrel containing a rather fragile-looking glass tube to hold the ink, but the pen produced in 1884 by L. E. Waterman was the first really practical one with many of the points of a modern pen. It was made of vulcanite and had a reservoir and controlled ink flow. Of course, this successful pen was followed by many others and, as with sewing machines, a great many fountain pens originated in the USA: Caw's Safety Fountain Pen ('when closed for the pocket, Caw's Safety Fountain Pen can be carried in any position in perfect safety') in the 1890s, in the early twentieth century Parker pens, Sheaffer pens and others—the Eagle Pencil Co. also in due course produced a more efficient writing instrument than the one mentioned above. In Britain, Mabie, Todd and Bard patented the Swan Pen—a name presumably given in honour of all the swan quills used in earlier times—and De La Rue the Pelican Self-Feeding Pen; 'Onoto, THE Pen' was advertised as being 'as British as the Pillar Box'. Swan pens cost from 10s. 6d. to £20 in 1902, and the Pelican in 1896 was 10s. 6d. Better quality pens had gold nibs which did not corrode, tipped with iridium for extra wear. A great drawback to many early fountain pens was their tiresome habit of leaking quantities of ink into the pocket unless they were kept

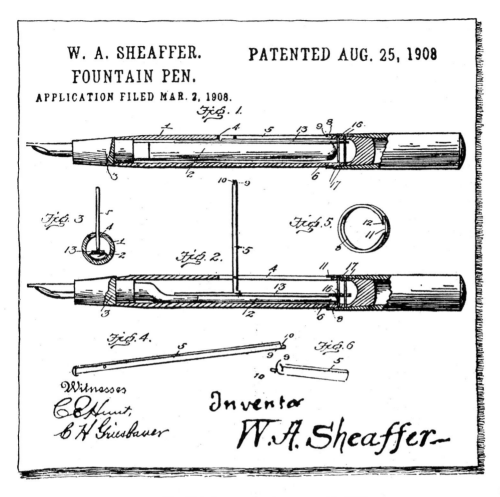

Sheaffer's lever mechanism patented in 1908

upright—even some which allegedly <u>could</u> not leak were not immune. For a woman, a silver case with repoussé decoration could be the answer, hung from the belt by a châtelaine hook—if by chance the pen did leak, the ink was at least contained. After the invention of the pen clip, men could keep it the right way up in a breast pocket. Prevention of leakages was one way in which pens were constantly being improved; the other main improvements were in methods of filling. At first this was done by means of a dropper with a rubber bulb—pens sold in presentation cases were often accompanied by one. This being a somewhat messy operation, efforts were made to overcome the difficulty and the self-filling pen was produced in the early twentieth century. W. A. Sheaffer in 1908 patented the first pen incorporating a lever device and many others followed. By the mid-1920s, Sheaffer, Parker and Onoto had progressed from lever to plunger-activated filling.

5
SMOKING

'It may be interesting to the public in general and more especially to the smoking section, to learn that the use of tobacco for smoking purposes within the precincts of Windsor Castle has been prohibited by the express command of Her Majesty the Queen. Cards, neatly framed and glazed requiring that gentlemen will not smoke in the Castle, have been hung in the private rooms of the Lords-in-Waiting and Equerries of the Royal Suite, and even in the rooms in the York Tower, which are being fitted up for H.R.H. the Prince of Wales. The servants and workmen of the Castle are also prohibited from smoking within the precincts of the Castle by command of Her Majesty' (*The Queen*, 1880).

Possibly a great many women would have liked to be able to carry matters with as high a hand as Queen Victoria, but, in default of this, smoking could sometimes be restricted to only a few rooms in the house, or, if space permitted, a special smoking-room could be set aside for the indulgence of this agreeable (to some) and mainly masculine vice. By this means, in one room only would the curtains and upholstery become permeated with stale tobacco smoke, which was undoubtedly a gain when heavy, non-washable hangings were fashionable and dry-cleaning a more lengthy and laborious process than today. Curtains throughout the house would still suffer from smoky fires and the fumes from gas chandeliers or oil lamps, but this was no doubt regarded as an unavoidable evil, which tobacco was not. In the smoking-room, especially, the Victorians (and Edwardians) went in for smoking in a big way, surrounding themselves with innumerable accessories, ranging from special costumes to extraordinary contraptions for lighting cigars and magnificent containers to hold them. Smoking jackets of velvet, often trimmed with braid in quasi-military style, kept tobacco smoke out of the ordinary coat, and smoking caps (often made and embroidered by the ladies of the family) kept it from the hair.

Pocket snuffbox in wood with silver trefoil inlay, late 19th century

Large beige silk snuff handkerchief, printed in black with scenes from the Crimean War. Wine border 1850s

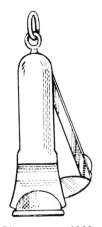

Cigar cutter c. 1900

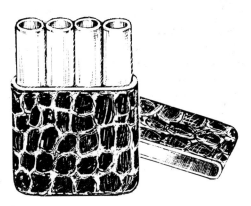

Cigar case with individual pockets 1907

The fashionable way of taking tobacco among the upper classes, during the early nineteenth century, had been as snuff and, although this became less fashionable, the habit by no means disappeared. It had its own necessary equipment: snuff boxes for the table and small boxes for the pocket, and also snuff handkerchiefs. All classes indulged in it to some extent throughout the nineteenth century—Mrs Gamp took snuff, but a luxurious silk snuff handkerchief, printed with a map of the Crimea and scenes from the war there, proves that it was still indulged in by the well-to-do. Coloured or printed handkerchiefs were preferred by snuff takers, as the stains were so hard to get out, and many were printed to commemorate famous events. However, cigars and cigarillos increasingly took the place of snuff and were the usual choice of the upper-class man until near the end of the century, when pipe smoking became more widespread. The lists of cigars available in, for instance, the Army and Navy Co-operative Society's catalogues make formidable reading, hundreds of different cigars being listed. At the Great Exhibition of 1851 many firms from many countries exhibited tobacco in all stages of manufacture as well as finished cigars.

While the changes in emphasis in fashionable society from snuff to cigars was taking place, the ordinary man continued to use a clay pipe, as he had done ever since tobacco was first introduced. One of the disadvantages of the clay was that it was porous and tended to stick to the lips:

'. . . Mr Vincent Crummles melting the sealing-wax on the stem of his pipe in the candle, and rolling it out afresh with his little finger' (*Nicholas Nickleby*, Charles Dickens).

This roll of sealing wax prevented sore lips and made for a more comfortable smoke. Later, the mouthpiece was lacquered or glazed. At the 1851 Exhibition William Southorn and Co., of Broseley, showed 'tobacco pipes, of prepared clay, which gives them a more porous quality; with improved glaze, and green lip'. This lip may have been treated to prevent the unpleasant sticking to the lip—anyway, Mr Southorn received an honourable mention. Other Victorian clay pipes sometimes have a pinkish mouthpiece, treated in imitation of the original wax.

Much more expensive, not to say luxurious, pipes were carved out of meer-schaum (Ger.=sea foam), a mineral mainly found in Turkey. Vienna became the chief source of elaborately carved pipe bowls of this material and, also in Vienna, they were fitted with amber mouthpieces. A Meerschaum pipe exhibited in 1851 by John Inderwick depicted the death of Nelson and was mounted with gold and silver. Unfortunately, these pipes, like the more expendable clays, had the disadvantage of being extremely fragile and the discovery of the Briar Pipe (made from the root of the Tree Heath or Bruyère of Corsica) made the other kinds almost redundant. Meerschaum pipes were, however, still made in the twentieth century, though mostly in more commonplace shapes—one of

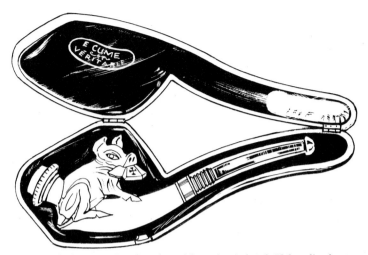

Meerschaum and amber pipe with comic pig bowl. Velvet-lined leather case, late 19th century

them costing around five times as much as a similar briar: about 15s. to 25s. for the meerschaum, while the briar would be about 3s. to 4s. Many briar pipes were made in shapes somewhat resembling the clay pipe; a 'reading' or 'garden' pipe was made that resembled the curved Churchwarden clay pipe, others had alternative long Albatross stems that could be fitted, to keep the smoke out of one's eyes.

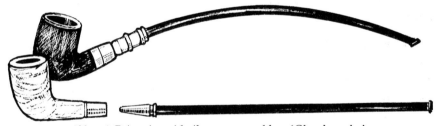

(Above) *Briar pipe with silver mount and long 'Churchwarden' type stem;* (Below) *garden or reading pipe with 'Albatross' stem*

It should not be supposed that smoking was at any time an exclusively masculine habit, even in Europe (in the East, it appears always to have been favoured by both sexes). Before the nineteenth century began, Madame Vigée le Brun was painted smoking a clay pipe and, although neither pipes nor cigars were much used by fashionable ladies, pipes in particular were regularly used by countrywomen. What really encouraged regular smoking by women (at first only in their boudoirs or in private with their friends) was the introduction of the cigarette. At the 1851 exhibition, only the Russians exhibited cigarettes, but their use rapidly spread, and in 1899 Neville Ainslie and Co. of Sloane Street, London, were advertising 'Cigarettes for Ladies. Specially selected mild Turkish'.

[87]

Silver case for matches or wax vestas 1883

Pig-shaped match container with bronze finish c. 1890

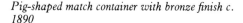

Some of the earliest brands on sale in Great Britain were Virginia, for instance Three Castles in 1878, the long-popular Woodbine in 1888, and Richmond Straight Cut Virginia cigarettes in 1884—'Cigarette smokers who are willing to pay a little more . . . will find them superior to all others'. But right up to the 1930s it was smarter (and more expensive) to smoke Turkish or Egyptian cigarettes; Abdulla Turkish, Balkan Sobranie, Pearls of Egypt are a few of the many brands imported, far outnumbering the Virginian brands advertised. Russian cigarettes with the card mouthpiece, for instance 'Troika' by Chapchal Frères, were also a fashionable choice. In the 1930s American cigarettes such as Lucky Strike, Camel (also in Turkish tobacco) and the menthol-cooled Spud became popular in Europe as well, and Virginia tobacco overtook all others in popularity.

By the 1920s ladies' cigarette cases and holders were being sold as well as men's, the cases sometimes combined with a vanity case and, by the end of the decade, cigarette holders were often extravagantly long. However, although it was now quite understood that women smoked—in fact there were many brands especially recommended—some women still considered it unladylike to smoke in public in the 1930s.

The injurious and addictive properties of nicotine do appear to have been already partially recognised in the nineteenth century: a cure for the smoking habit, called No-to-Bac was advertised in the USA in 1893 and, in the early twentieth century, patent cigarette holders with absorbent cartridges (the Montgomery Moore), or with a chamber for a cottonwool filter, were obtain-

(Above) *Long cigarette holder, cream with sapphire blue decoration 1925–30*

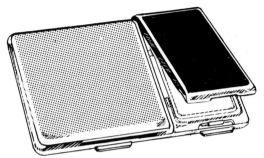

(Left) *Combined cigarette case and powder compact, chromium with red and black enamel 1935*

(Above) *The Montgomery Moore cigarette holder with filter against nicotine. 'The most effective Anti-Nicotine Holder invented' 1907*

(Left) *Lucky Strike cigarettes 1930*

able. Later, as the smoking habit became ever more widespread, the dangers were largely ignored and any apprehensions appear to have been considered a delusion of cranks and health faddists. An advertisement for Lucky Strike in 1930, in fact, suggests smoking as a help in slimming—if you feel tempted to have another chocolate, light up a 'Lucky' instead.

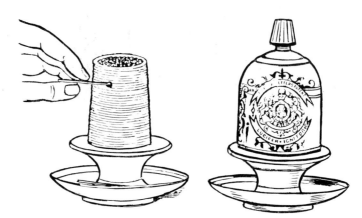

Loysel's Patent China Lucifer Match Ignitor, late 19th century

No Victorian or Edwardian smoking-room would have been complete without its elaborate cabinet with compartments for different kinds of cigar, a rack for pipes and a tobacco jar. Smokers' lamps—table lighters for cigars or pipes—were impressive affairs of 'antique' brass, or more graceful designs in silver, based on the old classical oil lamp. An electric lighter was to be had in 1898. But cheaper than all these was Loysel's Patent China Lucifer Match Ignitor (1s. and upwards), though it did put one to the trouble of striking a match (lucifer) instead of providing a constant flame. It could also of course be used for other purposes, including the melting of sealing wax. It was 'infallible, ornamental, durable and safe'.

The first pocket lighter was the Automatic Magic Pocket Lamp in 1890: 'opens and lights with one single pressure of the thumb'. Opening the lighter caused a spark by friction which, with luck, caught the tinder alight. Another kind, to be had in 1910 from Messrs Edwards and Sons in Regent Street, London, had a length of continuous tinder or wick which was fed through. But, on the whole, until the invention of the petrol lighter, it was safer to rely on matches and many small boxes for the pocket were made to take them.

For the pipe smoker, other important accessories were a pipe bowl scraper, for instance Terry's patent Hedgehog Pipe Reamer, and a pipe stopper; or perhaps the Combination Tobacco Stopper, Pricker and Cigar Holder in silver. Tobacco pouches of rubber or leather did not show much variation, but one of Austrian design, with a concertina base and the top unfolding like a flower, was much more attractive—indeed may still be made.

6
EXCURSIONS

Travelling

The nineteenth century was a period of great changes and upheavals, not least in methods of transport. The rapid development of the railways after 1830 produced easier and cheaper travel for a much larger number of people than ever before. It was, however, not necessarily more comfortable travel, though it was faster. Nowadays we are pampered by heated cars and railway coaches and, unless we have the misfortune to be snowed up, we forget that a journey in winter could be a bitter ordeal in horse-drawn vehicles and in the early trains. When the first motor-cars took to the road, they too were a particularly uncomfortable and cold means of transport, usually being open 'tourers', which left driver and passengers exposed to the elements, hardly less so than the outside passengers on a stage-coach—passengers were, in fact, described as travelling 'on' a motor-car, not 'in' one and special garments were designed to give protection from the elements. Draughty hoods and side curtains were complained of in an article in *Home Chat* in 1914, which enquired whether something better could not be devised; and although closed cars were available from 1918 it was not until after World War 2 that all cars were expected to have heaters installed.

For all except the hardiest, therefore, means of keeping warm were of very great importance. The earliest method (dating back to who knows when!) of keeping one's feet warm in a carriage was a heated brick (which, wrapped in flannel, was also sometimes used to warm beds). Later, portable foot warmers, of copper or tin, filled with hot water, were used, both in carriages and trains, and doubtless in cars as well. These warmers were usually covered with a strip of carpet or felt, which made them more comfortable to the feet and also had insulating properties. From the 1850s on, most railway companies made similar warmers available to passengers, either free or for a small charge. At least two

Muff or pocket hot water bottle, made by the Old Fulham Pottery, late 19th century

sorts of these warmers were made—the hot water ones, which cooled fairly rapidly, and an improved kind which burned a special slow-burning fuel, or a burning brick. Both kinds were remarkably similar in appearance. The 'Patent Instra' was a similar warmer of the early 1900s, using a patent fuel which was renewable. 'Instra' also marketed a small pocket or muff warmer, which could if necessary be hung inside the clothing. This small Instra was made of 'German Silver' (a nickel alloy), decoratively engraved and with a plush bag to keep it in. The large warmer was of polished copper, and cost 19s. 9d. with fifty refills, the Pocket Instra 7s. 3d. with refills. The Instra Warmer Co.'s motto was 'Warmth is Life'.

> 'To be warm, put the Instra in side pocket, to be warmer, hook it up just behind and below the hipbone and underneath the coat; if very chill and unwell, hook up on one or other side of the backbone.'

The pocket Instra had a chain and safety pin so that it could be fastened inside the clothing and:

> 'to air a damp bed quickly, put a chair in the bed, and the Instra inside'

(this being the large one, naturally). The refills were round sticks, about 5 in. (12·7 cm.) long for the small size, and covered in grey paper.

Damp bed detector. A useful hygrometer for travellers, early 20th century

With one or more warmers of this kind (there is a *Punch* cartoon of two travellers using five railway warmers apiece!) and a rug of a more or less

[92]

luxurious kind, journeys in cold weather were rendered less unendurable, and few Victorian or Edwardian travellers are pictured without a rug, usually strapped up, among their mounds of luggage. Carriage or motor rugs could be of fur, or rubberised against wet weather, but the travelling rug for train journeys was of thick, double-woven wool in tartan or check designs; the Eiderdown Rug, produced in the 1880s by Messrs Boyd and Co. of Belfast, was a cellular weave and highly praised in the columns of *The Queen*. It was not made of eiderdown—the Trades Description Act was as yet unheard of! A travelling rug was usually carried rolled up—two straps, joined by a handle, made a neat, easily carried parcel of it. Rugs for a carriage or car journey did not need to be so portable, and could be of a more luxurious kind—what could be finer than the quilted down motor wrap, with foot and hand muffs, to keep one warm in the chilly interior of an unheated limousine in 1925?

In Edwardian times, and probably earlier, some ladies, on the way to a dance, would wear knitted woolly boots over their thin shoes. The wearer had of course to remember to remove these unsightly objects when she took off her cloak—failure to do so was not unknown and the cause of great embarrassment to the wearer. In 1925, Glastonbury sheepskin overshoes for motoring were among the first to be made with Zip fasteners, in this case the Kynoch.

Heating was not the only lack in trains. Lighting also was for a long time poor or non-existent, and wise travellers took with them small candle-lamps to read by after dark, though these must have cast but a dim and flickering light in a rattling train. Without them, a journey after dark was a journey in the dark until the advent of gas and electric lighting in trains in about the 1870s and '80s (these gloomy conditions abruptly returned in World War 2, when the lighting in compartments was reduced to one faint glimmering bulb). Pairs of pack-away travelling candlesticks were also available, to use at ill-equipped inns beyond the range of civilisation and gas lighting.

A 'sensational discovery' in 1901, the dry battery torch, giving instant light 'when and where you want it', must have been a blessing indeed. No flickering, no danger of fire, and no fumbling in the dark with a box of matches—the Ever-Ready pocket torch provided portable electric light for the first time. A portable lamp and a battery-lit clock (the Shamrock) were also available—but

The Shamrock travelling clock with battery light
1902

[93]

of course it was necessary to carry spare batteries.

As there were no buffet or restaurant cars on trains until the end of the century, it was a wise precaution to arm oneself with the wherewithal for brewing-up and a container for food. True, at larger stations there were scheduled stops, where the passengers might dash out to find refreshment, but a portable case, containing spirit-stove, kettle, water, tea and other necessaries, avoided the possibility of being faced with the choice of abandoning the fight for sustenance or being left high and dry on the platform. Refreshment rooms, and platform vendors, would be overwhelmed by a sudden influx from a train and the weakest would go to the wall. These containers ranged from the little Sirram Traveller's Companion, measuring 6 in. × 5½ in. × 4½ in., to very much larger and more elaborate outfits, complete with crockery and cutlery. Drew's Patent En Route 5 o'clock Tea Basket (patented 1890) for two or four persons, which could be had with silver-plated fittings, had a top lid which could be turned back and slid into the grooves of a carriage window in order to hang the basket. The front could then be let down to form a table.

Telescopic metal tumbler with leather case, for travelling

From the 1870s, some railway companies (the first seems to have been the Midland line) provided hampers containing food and drink, the passenger paying for the contents and returning the empties. Vendors with trolleys carrying tea or coffee urns and other refreshments also did brisk business on platforms, purveying hot tea and buns, or lemonade. It is, in fact, not all that long ago that there were platform vendors at Waterloo Station, London, not to mention kiosks for magazines, papers and cigarettes, but these have now all been relegated to the general concourse, presumably because so many trains now have buffet cars.

Early trains not only had no buffet cars, they had no lavatories, and no corridors to reach them by, until the end of the nineteenth century and, on some trains, considerably later (some suburban trains still do not). Great self-control was essential and some people restricted their fluid intake for a time before a journey. For ladies who expected not to be able to hold out, Messrs Millikin and Lawley in 1873 advertised Ladies' Railway Conveniences. They also sold a Pocket Railway Key, said to open any railway carriage—there must have been fears at this period, well or ill-founded, of being locked in or out. Another help to travellers was the combined Leg-rest and Umbrella Holder, useful for putting one's feet up, always supposing that the seat opposite was not occupied. Presumably this was especially a boon to short-legged people who could not reach the opposite seat unaided.

The first Thermos flask was patented in 1902, and a very few years later this was to a great extent replacing the kettle which had to be boiled. The new invention was at first comparatively expensive, at over £1 a flask, and a case containing Thermos, crockery and cutlery might cost all of £5–£6, a considerable sum in those days. But by the middle of the 1920s the Sirram Traveller's

Thermos flask 1920s

Companion had risen in price to 10s., nearly double that in 1900, while the increasingly popular Thermos flask had halved in price. Many similar flasks came on the market at even lower prices—in the 1930s a vacuum flask could be bought for about 3s. 6d. By this time any flask of this type was called a 'Thermos', a word being added to the English language, in the same way that 'Hoover' and hoovering eventually came to be applied to any vacuum cleaner. By the 1930s the Thermos had for some years been available in a variety of shapes and sizes, including a wide-mouthed jar for soups and stews.

Luggage

'A young lady's trunk was a trunk in those days. Now it is a two or three storied edifice of wood in which two or three full grown bodies of young ladies (without crinoline) might be packed. I saw a little old countrywoman at the Folkestone station last year with her travelling baggage contained in a bandbox . . . and she surveyed Lady Knightsbridge's twenty-three black trunks, each wellnigh as large as her ladyship's opera box . . . dumbly' (*Adventures of Philip*: W. M. Thackeray).

Thackeray may have been exaggerating but, of necessity, luggage from the

[95]

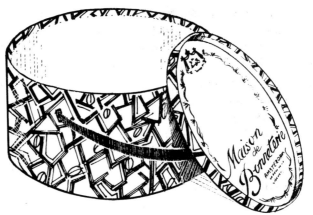

Miniature bandbox printed gold and black. Used as packaging by the 'Maison de Bonneterie', The Hague and Amsterdam, in the 1920s and 30s

mid-nineteenth century to the early twentieth was much more cumbersome than we are used to today—the countrywoman's bandbox would in fact seem much more normal and reasonable than the mounds of baggage taken by well-to-do people for even relatively short stays away from home. Fashionable dresses, and indeed all female garments, contained large quantities of material, what with crinoline petticoats and the wide skirts, sometimes containing six widths of material, to go over them, flounces, linings, trains in the 1870s and 1880s, and, in addition, far more changes of clothes and underclothes than we would think were necessary, because of the difficulties of washing and drying. Chemises, petticoats, combinations, drawers, corset covers, of linen or long-cloth—and all to our eyes of a totally unnecessary size—could not be rinsed through quickly and put on again the following day, and even for a short stay a woman would need to take enough clothes for a good-sized case. A lady going to a country house-party would also be obliged to take clothes for several changes during the day—for morning, for afternoon tea, for dinner, not to mention walking or riding, shooting or boating, or whatever other activities were likely to engage her. Obviously, several trunks, valises and hatboxes were necessary! Men's luggage was also often formidable, though not on quite such a scale.

Dress trunks (or dress 'baskets') were frequently made on a wicker framework covered with waterproofed canvas. The lid was domed and covered a tray at the top which was sometimes divided into sections, this part taking accessories and the lower portion the dresses. More substantial trunks were of wood, covered with leather and studded with round-headed nails, or of japan-ned tin, often oak-grained or a serviceable olive-green. A more expensive form of the metal trunk was made of steel and either of these could be reinforced with wooden bars. These metal trunks or tin-lined ones were essential for voyagers to the tropics. Tin trunks had the advantage, too, of being cheap.

The Queen's Era Combinati trunk (1898) was made to carry hats in its tray,

[96]

but, in general, special hat or bonnet boxes would be used—bonnet boxes in japanned metal to carry one or more bonnets and, at the end of the century and during the Edwardian era, enormous round or square boxes to take the gigantic hats. These boxes usually had small humps of horse hair or wire gauze fixed inside to which the hats could be pinned. This prevented movement in transit, which was very damaging to hats lavishly trimmed with flowers, ribbons or feathers—or all three. Men's hat boxes were usually leather bucket-shaped cases, to fit the essential top hat and possibly one other. Larger square cases in 1900 (and onwards) had fittings and straps to carry top hat, bowler, opera hat (collapsible) and a boater. In contrast to this, a small case about 14 in. × 4 in. (35·5 cm × 10 cm) would just carry a boater.

Three kinds of case are especially associated with Victorian times: the Compendium or dressing box, the Carpet Bag, and the Gladstone Bag.

The Compendium was essentially a product of the age of coach travel—a means of having easy access to anything that might be needed on the journey. These boxes or caskets were fitted out with small personal accessories, such as sewing tools, cosmetic jars and other toilet articles, and usually had a padded tray for jewellery. A writing desk could also be incorporated, but was usually carried as a separate item. Lift-out trays, or drawers, gave access to the lower tiers of implements, a mirror was held in the lid cavity, and there were sometimes secret drawers and compartments to hold money and other valuables. The example illustrated on page 107 came from Héber of Palais Royale, Paris, and was particularly well fitted out. It is of burr walnut bound with brass.

After rail travel became the norm, the usefulness of dressing boxes diminished: they were inconvenient to carry and, as against a private coach, there was no convenient place to put them in the train. All the same they continued to be made and, no doubt, used. A compendium by Asprey's, described in *The Queen* in 1868, was an extraordinary article, an example of conspicuous consumption rather than utility. It was of coromandel wood*, with a set of cut-glass jars and bottles, with silver-gilt tops studded with carbuncles set in pearls. All the fittings had silver-gilt mounts and many were in duplicate. In addition to other delights, it had many 'cleverly arranged secret contrivances for letters, gold, and bank notes'.

For rail travel, they were increasingly replaced by leather fitted dressing cases, which, though larger, were more convenient to carry and held considerably more. The many dressing boxes which survive have usually lost most of their original contents and now serve the purpose of a work box. A twentieth-century descendant of these boxes appeared in 1914 in the form of a Motor Companion with a roll-top, containing mirror, jars, scissors etc. and with

---

* Coromandel wood: from the tree *Diospyros quaesita* (syn. *hirsuta*?) related to Ebony and the Persimmon tree. It grows in Ceylon and on the Coromandel coast (South East India).

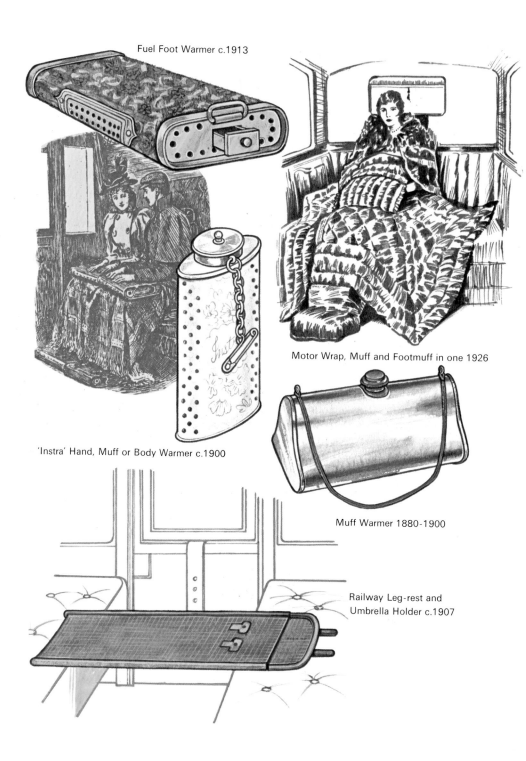

Fuel Foot Warmer c.1913

'Instra' Hand, Muff or Body Warmer c.1900

Motor Wrap, Muff and Footmuff in one 1926

Muff Warmer 1880-1900

Railway Leg-rest and Umbrella Holder c.1907

Drew's 'En Route' 5 o'clock Tea Basket 1891

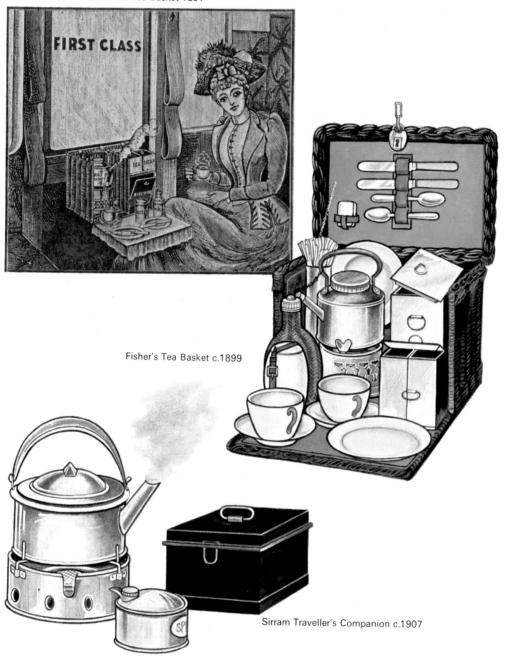

FIRST CLASS

Fisher's Tea Basket c.1899

Sirram Traveller's Companion c.1907

a clock on its face. This 'novelty' (obtainable from the Goldsmiths and Silver-smiths Company) could be had in grey wood, with fitments in soft grey leather and silver-gilt bordered with sapphire blue enamel; or in different woods and colourings to match your car exactly—obviously designed for the luxury trade, as were the boxes described above.

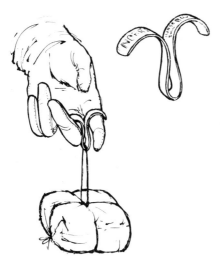

Parcel carrier free to customers. Inscribed 'Morris's Horse-skin Boots'

The Carpet Bag was, as its name says, made out of a strip of carpet and had a leather mount and handle, sometimes a lock. Usually, but not always, it had side gussets. As hand luggage, with the rest of the baggage in the van, as an overnight case, or as the only piece taken by those too poor to own more, it was equally useful, cheap and hardwearing, and lighter than a leather case. Its heyday was the middle of the nineteenth century—it is often depicted in paintings of that period, and in many Victorian novels the hero in a hurry travels with only a carpet bag.

The earliest mention of a Gladstone Bag (named after the statesman) was in May 1869 in the *Englishwoman's Domestic Magazine* and spoke of it as a novelty, but the description given does not seem altogether to tally with the bag usually known by this name:

> 'It is made in black enamelled or brown cowhide. It expands sufficiently to contain a gentleman's wardrobe for a fortnight's use, or can be used small enough to hold only the necessities for one day's use.'

The bag usually opened down the middle and could be obtained either plain or fitted as a dressing case. It was still used well into the twentieth century.

Expanding cases were being made as long ago as 1868, when H. J. Cave and Sons of Edwards Street, Portman Square, London, submitted a specimen to *The Queen* for comment. It is described as a 'packing trunk of extraordinary capacity, with a handled tray... the top of this trunk is capable of great

[100]

expansion, being fitted with a bellows-like arrangement of leather'. Many others were made on this principle. But in 1921 and 1923 the special fastenings were patented which were used in the popular Revelation Suitcase. This was made on quite a new principle—it had a deep lid and long hinges and clasps which worked on a ratchet. When pulled up to the highest point, the case could take nearly double its capacity when fully closed.

Wardrobe Trunks were particularly useful for long sea voyages or cruises. An early one was patented in England in 1893. The set of matching Wardrobe Trunk and other cases was produced in 1930 by Oshkosh of Oshkosh, Minnesota, one of the top manufacturers of luxury cases in the USA. In Europe, at this time, 'Top People' usually chose luggage by Louis Vuitton of Paris. A Vuitton case of the 1920s to 1930s can be recognised by its solidity and its covering of brown with all-over design of fleur-de-lys.

Suitcases, fitted dressing cases, and entire sets of matching luggage in the upper price ranges, were made of leather, cowhide or pigskin. These were fantastically heavy compared to present-day cases, but were used (by those who could afford them) up to World War 2, because there was then seldom any lack of porters at railway stations to do the carrying and, as flying was the exception, there was no need to worry about excess weight. The great increase in travel by air undoubtedly was important in bringing about modern lightweight cases.

Walking

Long, full, and sometimes trained, skirts were one of the obstacles that had to be overcome by women who had to, or who wished to, walk out-of-doors any

Wooden pattens with leather strap and iron ring, mid 19th century

[101]

Lawn Tennis Shoes in Black French Kid 1878

Paul's Patent Mittens
for the Feet 1906

The 'Queen Anne'
Lawn Tennis Shoes 1878

Sealskin Gaiters 1890s

Spats 1920

Ladies Rubber
Wellington Boots

Galoshes 1850-60

Japanese Paper Parasol 1920s

Parasol with Leather Handle/Case, early 1900s

The 'Winefride'
Umbrella Handle
c.1874

Walking-length Parasol c.1875

Combined Umbrella and Stick c.1890s

[103]

distance; they were particularly an encumbrance because of the dirt in the streets in the nineteenth century. In town, there were the crossing-sweepers (such as Jo in *Bleak House*: Charles Dickens), wretched boys or men who earned a few pence a day in this way; but they were not always on hand to clear the dirt away for a lady wishing to cross the road. Working women or countrywomen, who anyway usually wore stouter boots or shoes, had recourse to pattens, both out-of-doors or when doing work in the wash house or other wet work, and these raised the hems of dresses clear of mud, as well as protecting shoes. But by the middle of the nineteenth century pattens were not much favoured by ladies taking the air in town and, indeed, must always have been inconvenient for walking any distance.

Before the middle of the century, rubber goloshes were available—in c. 1839 a pair cost about 6s. 6d. ('a pair of India-rubber goloshes that cost six-and-sixpence'—*Nicholas Nickleby*: Charles Dickens). Goloshes were shown at the Great Exhibition in 1851, similar to those shown on page 102; and production on a commercial scale began in 1859. They were not then, and never became, objects of beauty, though immensely practical. They never became fashionable for the same reason, and also because they did indicate, so very plainly, that the

Men's goloshes 1926

wearer actually had to walk—had no carriage to take her on her errand. Mrs Haweis (*The Art of Beauty*, 1883) protested at their ugliness—'Ah, woe be to that man who invented the gutta-percha penance' and at feet 'swelled to unnatural proportions by the hideous golosh' and recommended that instead women should revert to pattens, not the nineteenth-century model but one based on the much earlier one as painted by Jan van Eyck in the *Arnolfini Wedding*.

Some goloshes were more efficient than others. In 1897, the 'waist foothold golosh' was advertised by O'Brien's Patents Ltd, which avoided wet boots and therefore 'death from colic, catarrh, sore throat and peritonitis!' Getting wet feet was, for nineteenth-century heroines, a sure precursor of illness, decline or death. If correspondence in the *Englishwoman's Domestic Magazine* is to be trusted, it seems that there was, in the 1870s, a strong movement in favour of allowing children, at any rate, to go barefoot—it was not wet feet that mattered, but going around with wet shoes and stockings; and shoes were the cause of corns and deformities.

Different styles of golosh developed, not much less hideous than the early ones—in the 1920s a half-golosh, which covered only the toe, and was worn with high heels. Another one was the ankle-length rubber overboot with fur trimming. The shiny black high boots called Wellingtons were more popular for country wear.

Rubber was used for soles for boots and shoes by 1850. Not only men but women too became addicted to the fashionable new game of Lawn Tennis in 1870, and it was discovered that a rubber-soled shoe was less liable to slip on grass than ordinary footwear. In spite of this small improvement, it was still a relatively tame game, as most women players wore their ordinary long skirts, sometimes with a train, and of course a hat or bonnet. Men came off rather better in this respect. One female tennis shoe was the Watteau, or Queen Anne, shoe, registered in 1878. Made in patent leather [!] or kid, it had an ankle strap and a corrugated sole and cost 14s. 6d., post free from the sole maker, Samuel Winter of Queen's Gate, London.

Another way to keep feet and ankles warm, if not dry, was to wear gaiters. Fashionable boots and shoes, especially in the late nineteenth century were, for both men and women, very narrow and pointed and must have made for cold feet—when wearing shoes the ankles would suffer. The answer was gaiters; felt or woollen cloth in drab brown and greys were the usual kind, but sealskin or other flat furs were the best for those who could afford them—sealskin was in fact a very fashionable fur from the 1860s on. As for men, tough leather gaiters or leggings were worn by countrymen and for shooting. Spats (which are in fact ankle-length gaiters) were standard wear in town from 1890 up to the 1930s; linen ones were often worn in summer.

Skirt Lifters or Porte-jupes

A pair of goloshes, though protecting the feet, did nothing at all to keep the skirt out of the dirt and crinoline skirts were often fitted with an internal arrangement of loops and cords which could be used to pull up the skirt all round. This is often seen in photographs of the 1860s, particularly of ladies on the croquet lawn (croquet was a very popular game); and for a time it was fashionable for 'fast' young ladies to pull up their gowns in this way and display their (often scarlet) petticoats and their natty boots when out walking. Useful though it no doubt was, this arrangement could not easily be adapted for use with the dresses of the 1870s and 1880s, which were worn over bustles or tightly swathed round the hips and often had trains. During this period several kinds of skirt lifter were designed, which gripped the skirt or train and were lifted by a cord or chain.

The model patented by Fyfe's in 1876 worked on the principle of a pair of

Tin Travelling Trunk 1907

'Queen's Era' Combination
Dress and Millinery Trunk 1898

Oshkosh Wardrobe Trunk, Suitcase and Golf Bag 1930

Bonnet Box 1881, with Hat 1884

Compendium from Héber, Paris, c.1860

Box for Two Small Bonnets 1880s

[107]

tongs, with the ends protected by pads of rubber to prevent damage to the dress and a sliding cast bronze butterfly clasp which pulled up to hold the tongs closed. A pull on the attached cord would raise the hem. Other designs for the sliding clasp were also made and often there was a 'châtelaine' hook on the cord or chain. Another form of Porte-jupe, in white metal, had a spring clip and locking device and was probably less kind to the skirt. Miller Brothers, of Newgate Street, London, sold a Lever-lock Dressholder said to be 'especially suitable for valuable and delicate materials' in 1880. But the one with probably the strongest grip of all was another Fyfe's patent (1880), which had a particularly strong spring and a cast bronze ornament on the front. This was lifted by a chain to a bangle on the wrist, so that the wearer only had to raise her arm.

Needless to say none of these inventions could lift a skirt all round as the crinoline skirt had been raised; with a trained dress, and many even of the walking dresses of the 1870s had trains, usually the only practicable method was to lift the train over the arm, or hold it up by a loop of material provided for the purpose—this was very often found on ball dresses, to make it possible to dance! There were many complaints about the filthy habit of women sweeping the streets with their dresses and the justice of these is borne out by the condition of some hems. Skirts were generally edged with a tough woollen braid to give some protection, or with a springy 'brush-braid' which must literally have swept the street or the carpet. Mrs Beeton lists as one of the duties of a lady's maid 'during the winter and in wet weather, the dresses should be carefully examined and the mud removed' (*Book of Household Management*). Some of this mud would no doubt have been thrown up by carriage wheels.

Most of the contraptions listed above seem rather doubtfully efficient gadgets; but one American skirt lifter, fixed inside the skirt, may have been rather more effective. This was Blackwood's Magic Skirt Elevator—'it is quickly changed to any dress and lifts and loops it fashionably with one easy pull: it lowers itself'—but it does seem to have been useful only for overskirts.

Coping with a long skirt had its difficulties, which were not made any the less by probably having one's hands occupied also with muff, reticule and umbrella, if it was raining, or a parasol if the sun was shining—this was a vital part of the defences against suntan. Although Fox metal frames were becoming usual in the mid-nineteenth century, for both umbrellas and parasols, cheaper ones were still made with cane spokes and the previously common whalebone was not unknown. Small parasols in the 1860s still often had folding sticks (in fashion plates these are shown more often in this decade than any other) and could be carried folded in the hand, but usually there was also a carrying ring by which it could be carried when closed, this being at what today would be the ferrule end. Black lace over white silk was very fashionable. Another method of keeping off the sun, especially at the seaside, was to wear what was called an 'ugly'. These were introduced at the end of the '40s, when bonnet brims became too small to shield the face adequately. Uglies were made of hoops of cane under silk covers, and were tied on over the bonnet brim.

In the 1870s they vanished, probably because by then bonnets had retreated so far to the back of the head that there was no longer any brim to tie them to, and in any case those women who engaged in outdoor pursuits would be more likely to be wearing hats worn forward over the forehead. This decade saw the return of larger sunshades, of walking length, still, often, with the walking handle at what, to us, would be the wrong end. Men's umbrellas, however, always seem to have had the handle at the same end, whether open or closed. For women, the bother of carrying either an umbrella or a parasol could be circumvented by the use of the Winefride Umbrella Handle (1874), which, it was said, could be fixed to any umbrella and was hung from a belt. As it looked somewhat like a sword hilt, it gave a distinctly martial air. In 1881, an economically-minded woman could convert her umbrella into a sunshade when required, by means of the Penelope Sun Umbrella Cover. According to the makers, 'the novelty of this cover consists of its capability of being adjusted to four different sizes of umbrella'. In white or cream satin with different colour bindings, it could be removed for washing.

From this time on, parasols (and umbrellas) increased steadily in size and those for garden parties and other important functions were lavishly trimmed, not only as regards the outer cover, but often the lining as well. Very tall umbrellas, too high for comfortable support when walking, were the fashion in about 1912, but were replaced in the '20s and '30s by stumpy umbrellas that were carried under the arm, or in outsize handbags. Japanese paper parasols were also very popular in the '20s, and very much used at seaside places, before a suntanned skin was regarded with general favour. Not all parasols of 1910–20 were tall; there were many types of folding umbrella, including the one from Vickery's of Regent Street, London, that folded away into its own green leather handle. Folding, or otherwise surprising brollies, were not a female prerogative: a man's walking stick, c. 1890s, could be telescoped together and removed to display the slimmest-ever rolled silk umbrella, and other canes housed revolvers, pencils, swords, cigarettes, or other useful accessories. The Cunliffe Shooting Seat in 1914 (for men and women) could be adapted in a minute to form an umbrella. This was sold by Mappin and Webb, and cost 33s. 6d.

Owing to the new popularity of sunbathing and the desirability of a tan, parasols, except for the occasional or purely decorative accessory, went into eclipse in the '20s, but elderly ladies still used their large Edwardian-style shades, especially in the country, and many an umbrella stand still held (and in some cases still does hold) a large faded object in floral chintz or green linen.

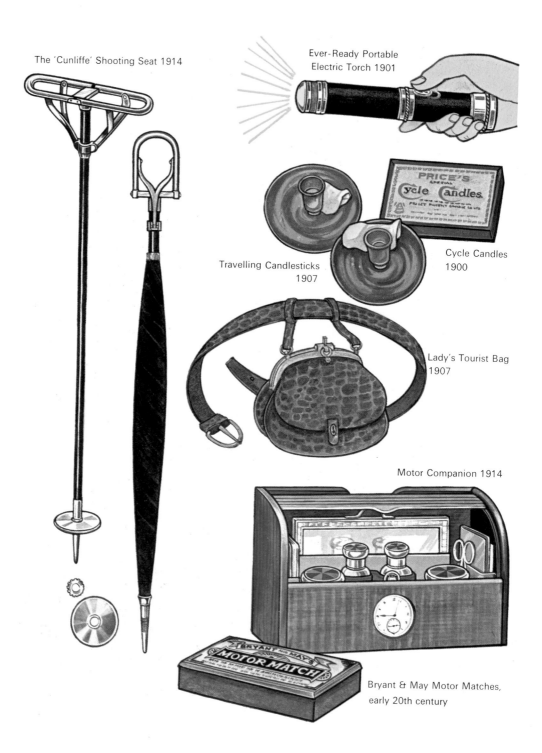

The 'Cunliffe' Shooting Seat 1914

Ever-Ready Portable Electric Torch 1901

Travelling Candlesticks 1907

Cycle Candles 1900

Lady's Tourist Bag 1907

Motor Companion 1914

Bryant & May Motor Matches, early 20th century

Skirt Lifter (with Bangle) 1880

Skirt Lifter 1876

Skirt Lifter 1876

Cap Basket 1870s

Fisher's Gladstone Bag c.1887

Carpet Bag 1850-60

[111]

7
CHILDREN

In Victorian England, the children in upper class and wealthy families at least, lived in almost a separate world to that of the adults.

> 'The nursery is of great importance in every family, and in families of distinction, where there are several young children, it is an establishment kept apart from the rest of the family, under the charge of an upper nurse, assisted by nursery maids' (Mrs Isabella Beeton, c. 1865).

A day and a night nursery were usual, but more room would be necessary for a very large family and there could be a whole nursery floor. A decline in infant mortality, due mainly to slightly improved hygiene, at least in the middle and upper classes, and of course no family planning, meant that families of ten or more were the rule rather than the exception and it was perhaps no wonder that the mother, so often probably 'in a delicate situation', should relegate her family to another's care. In many of the 'families of distinction' in Britain, the children might only see their mother for an hour or so a day and Mrs Beeton continues:

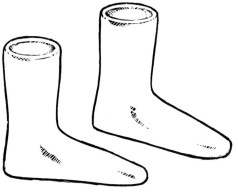

White-glazed pottery sock dryers, mid 19th century

'the children's hour should be an institution in every household'. She castigates 'women of fashion living constantly in society who will not take this time from gaiety and pleasure, to devote it to their children'. In neither the rest of Europe nor in the USA was the division of parents from children, as a rule, carried to such lengths.

Nearly all babies in the nineteenth century were breastfed; and, during this time, even the 'woman of fashion' referred to by Mrs Beeton would have to spend time with her baby; unless for any reason she could not feed it, and then, in well-off families, it was usual to employ a wet-nurse. 'Bringing up by hand', the Victorian expression for bottle-rearing, was, according to an American physician, so often a failure because neither mothers nor nurses (nor, it seems, most doctors) appreciated the quantity or quality of milk required by an infant, cow's milk being frequently diluted by up to twice its quantity of water:

'Who has not seen the poor little emaciated child of rich parents . . . never ceasing its low and plaintive moan, gradually passing away for ever? . . . there is little difficulty in raising children by hand if they are allowed a full supply of good milk' (c. 1869).

Children of the poor were sometimes better off 'by a habit which prevails among the poor, of giving it, while the mother is eating, small bits of bread or biscuit soaked in coffee'. Small wonder that a wet-nurse was considered the better alternative. By the 1870s, however, this custom was being increasingly abandoned, except in cases where the family doctor considered it really necessary. Mrs Beeton, for one, maintained that it was better to rear a child on cow's or goat's milk, rather than hire a nurse, her main objection being that 'conscientiousness and good faith' were rarely found in nurses who had undertaken the job primarily from the admittedly laudable motive of earning enough to feed their own families—the nurse's baby being of course fed the cow's milk, over-diluted or not, on which the employer's child did not thrive. A better knowledge of nutrition, and the manufacture of more sophisticated baby foods (Allen and Hanbury's Food was patented in 1891), virtually eliminated the employment of wet-nurses.

Babies' bottles in the mid-nineteenth century were still mostly of the flat flask or boat-shaped kind, made of pottery or glass, with a very small mouthpiece, and a larger hole on the top of the body which was used both for filling the bottle and for controlling the flow of milk by the mother's or nurse's thumb; the pottery bottles were sometimes handsomely transfer-printed Staffordshire wares. This type of bottle was still supplied by Maw's in 1907, in glass, but by then with a teat and stopper. Upright bottles were not unknown, with the large opening in the side, and a pear-shaped bottle of thick coloured glass, made by Matthew Tomlinson and sold at 1s., was advertised as 'well adapted to the working man's household'. As glass became cheaper, pottery bottles were no longer made; clear glass also had the great advantage over pottery in that it was

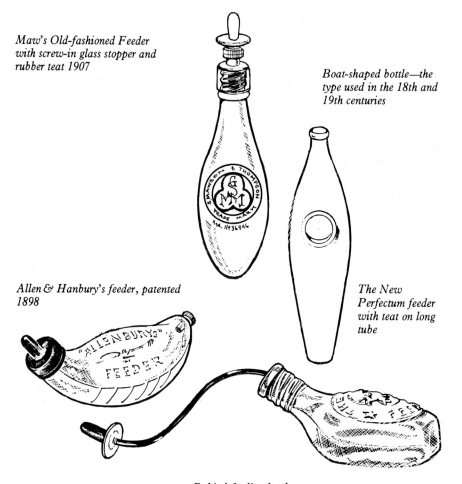

Maw's Old-fashioned Feeder with screw-in glass stopper and rubber teat 1907

Boat-shaped bottle—the type used in the 18th and 19th centuries

Allen & Hanbury's feeder, patented 1898

The New Perfectum feeder with teat on long tube

Babies' feeding bottles

easier to keep clean, though the full importance of this was as yet only imperfectly appreciated. Rubber teats were patented in New York as early as the 1840s, but this early rubber had an objectionable smell and taste which made it unpopular with babies and their parents alike and it was not, therefore, until this problem had been overcome that teats came into general use. By the time that the Cleanfont Nipple, catalogued by Fox, Fulte and Co. in the USA in the 1890s, was being made, the quality had greatly improved. The Cleanfont was also ribbed inside and could not collapse.

A most remarkable bottle was noticed in 1869, in the *Englishwoman's Domestic Magazine*—the Mama Bottle:

'The very best substitute for Mama herself is the "Mama" Feeding Bottle; and on seeing it I cannot help wondering that it was not thought of before, so simple, so beautiful, so <u>natural</u> is the mechanism. The bottle consists of two parts, made large enough to admit the entrance of the hand to clean them out. The fore part of

[114]

the "Mama" bottle is composed of india-rubber, offering a soft cushion to the little cheek of the babe; the form is that of the natural breast, and is readily accepted by infants who refuse to touch the ordinary feeding bottle.'

A flattened gourd-shaped glass bottle called the New Perfectum had a screw-in glass top with a rubber washer and teat. This type was common in the late nineteenth century, and still on sale in 1907. Similar ones were the Syphonia, the Alexandra, and in the USA the Barr's Patent, all these having the teat on the end of a long rubber tube—these needed, therefore, no holding in the case of an older baby (most babies were weaned on to solid food much later than nowadays).

A new shape was patented in 1898 by Allen and Hanbury's, which had a teat and a valve—being open at both ends it could be flushed through under the tap and it had no corners for deposits to be trapped in. Also, 'there is no tube to breed germs', and it had other advantages. This was by far the most popular shape during the early twentieth century, though in about the early 1930s an upright bottle became popular again.

Baby food could be prepared and warmed-up in Clarke's Pyramid Food Warmer, which was a china receptacle on a metal stand, with a nightlight to provide the heat. These little heaters were also useful for keeping drinks hot for invalids.

White silk layette pin cushion, with design stuck in pins, mid 19th century

Much suffering must have been inflicted by the careless use of pins, before the invention of the safety pin; nurses and mothers were advised to use as few as possible and to use tapes instead wherever possible. One of the items in a layette used to be a pincushion, with the pins arranged in fancy patterns or spelling out a greeting such as 'Welcome, little stranger'. Originally a practical gift, these cushions finally became a merely decorative adjunct to a baby's paraphernalia and the pattern of pins was rarely disturbed. They were presented as a gift after the birth and were usually of white silk or satin, embroidered and lace-trimmed. The Danish safety pin was not introduced into England until 1878, but safety

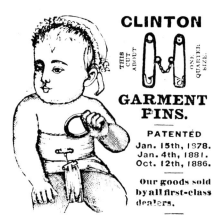

CLINTON

GARMENT
PINS.

PATENTED
Jan. 15th, 1978.
Jan. 4th, 1881.
Oct. 12th, 1886.

Our goods sold
by all first-class
dealers.

THIS CUT ABOUT ONE QUARTER SIZE.

pins of a kind were available earlier—the Nursery Favorite Safety Pin was patented in New York in 1871, and was said to be 'the best and most perfect pin ever made' with the point fully protected when closed. In 1879 there was the improved safety pin:

> 'Why make baby cry by using "safety" pins badly made of common wire when for 6d per box or 1s. per card you can buy GOODMAN'S royal silver SAFETY PINS which are entirely nickel silver . . . and cannot bend or become unfastened?'

But it was not until the early twentieth century that the curved nappy safety pin was invented, which really made it easy to pin a nappy without stabbing the baby.

On the other hand, with the Eureka Diaper from the USA there was no necessity for any pins, as it buttoned on over the muslin nappy and held it in place.

The next hurdle in the Victorian infant's path was, in most cases, teething: 'convulsion fits often follow the feverish restlessness produced' (Mrs Beeton again). The traditional coral was still generally used for babies to cut their teeth on:

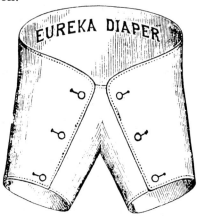

EUREKA DIAPER

The buttoning Eureka Diaper, USA 1880s

'"Not got a coral! Not got a coral!—how can you expect that he should cut his teeth? have you got Daffy's Elixir?" Eleanor explained that she had not. It had not been ordered by Mr Rerechild' (*Barchester Towers*: Anthony Trollope).

The smooth hardness of coral was supposed to be ideal for the purpose, though teething rings were also made of ivory, vegetable ivory (from Corozo nuts), amber or ebony, which had similar qualities. The tradition of using coral was a very old one, originally perhaps stemming from its ancient reputation as a protection against the Evil Eye. Coral has been associated with children in other ways than teething sticks or rings, often being used for their ornaments; in the

Coral and chain necklace for a small girl

1860s and '70s a lady calling herself Lavinia advertised that she made coral brooches, chains, bracelets etc., and 'infants' coral necklets and shoulder knots'; and coral necklaces were still given to small girls in the 1920s and '30s (and probably still are), though the ancient superstition about its protective properties was long forgotten.

Daffy's Elixir, mentioned above, might have been considered old-fashioned in 1857. It was first compounded by Anthony (or Thomas) Daffy in about 1700, and an eighteenth-century recipe for it includes liquorice, senna, rhubarb, carraway seeds and other ingredients. It was good for the colic and 'it purgeth two or three times a day'—too much, one would suppose, for an infant. Though not specifically a child's remedy, it is several times mentioned in connection with children. It was, in the nineteenth century, put up in a dark bottle with Daffy's name in raised letters; and it was to be bought up to 1931!

Teething sticks or rings, of whatever material, were very often combined with the baby's rattle, the most elaborate article of this kind being a silver rattle with chased decoration, hung with silver bells and with a handle of coral. They were the playthings of babies and young children for generations—a rattle is shown in a seventeenth-century portrait that is not so very different from the one illustrated here. These, however, were expensive toys; a cheaper kind had a wooden handle and the bells sewn on to leather strips (c. 1920). Ivory rings had a bell, or an attachment which rattled; globular hollow wooden rattles filled with dried peas also made a satisfactory amount of noise, and from the 1890s

[117]

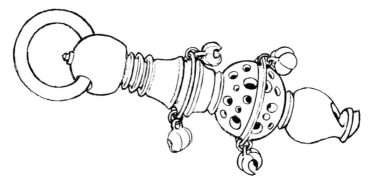

Baby's rattle, teething ring and whistle combined, made of vegetable ivory and silver, mid-19th century

this kind was made of a new material, celluloid, although this was very inflammable and the cause of many accidents. Older children had celluloid dolls and, above all, celluloid ducks and boats to float in the bath.

Afterwards, when the children were in bed, any fears of the dark could be countered by one of Price's or Clarke's nightlights.

(Left) *Nightlight saucer by Clarke, early 20th century;* (Right) *glass holder for Venus nightlight*

'When nights are dark then think of Clarke,
    Who's hit the mark precisely.
For his Night-lights create light nights,
    In which you see quite brightly.'

Where a fully separate nursery system was established, the children would also have most of their meals there, though this varied from family to family—in some, the children would join their parents at least for the midday meal. Nursery meals would be supervised by Nanny or the governess. The baby who had been promoted to a high chair at table had also by the 1920s a special high-bordered plate so that food was not pushed on to the table, and the baby of about 1907 was also sometimes provided with the helpful 'pusher' as well as a spoon. These could be among the christening presents, of which the foremost was usually a silver mug (very similar sometimes to mugs one hundred or more years older). The christening mug, if valuable, was probably <u>not</u> used for nursery tea.

[118]

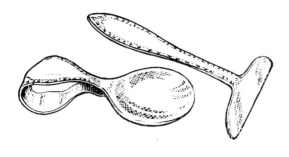

(Left) *Infant's spoon and pusher, plate 1928*
(Right) *Christening mug 1928*

Learning

For the first steps in learning, whether at home or school, a slate was commonly used, as it could so easily be wiped and used over and over again, until it met the usual fate of slates and got broken. In some village schools it would be used even by older children, where the expense of exercise books could not be met.

The development of handwriting was considered most important, and once a child had mastered its letters it would be set to copy out lines of orthodox copybook writing with thick and thin ups and downs. Another aid to good handwriting was the writing slope, or portable desk, or of course the sloping school desk; and there was the Lamson Pen and Hand Support made by J. E. Jenkins and Co., Massachusetts, USA, for 25 cents, which 'enables everyone to hold the pen correctly when writing—does not cramp hand. Every child needs it' (c. 1890).

FOR SCHOOL CHILDREN.

The Lamson PEN and Hand Support.

Enables every one to hold the pen correctly when writing. Does not cramp the hand. Every one can use it. Every child needs it. Send **25c.** for sample, stating your age, that we may send the right size.
J. E. JENKINS & CO., 156 Market St., Lynn, Mass.

(Above) *Learning to write with the Lanson Aid 1890s*

(Left) *Child's slate, with slate pencil and sponge for cleaning 19th century*

Older children took their books and pencil case to school in a satchel—they have done this for some four hundred and fifty years. Education at home for younger children was helped along by simple spelling and figuring aids, and alphabets, geographical and historical dissected (jigsaw) puzzles, and other didactic toys. The Victorians were never prone to let an educational opportunity go by, even in a game, and even Snakes and Ladders turned up in moral and improving forms.

Wooden teaching and picture blocks, Marshall Field & Co. USA 1892

Toys in the Nursery

For little girls, the first plaything would almost certainly be a doll, at first an unbreakable wooden or rag doll. Rag dolls were sold in the twentieth century by, amongst others, Dean's Manufacturing Co., and Sunny Jim, also a rag doll, could be obtained until recently from the makers of Force Breakfast Wheat Flakes. The sometimes very expensive wax or bisque dolls were in many families considered far too valuable and fragile for uninhibited play and the doll would be kept wrapped safely in a cupboard except for strictly rationed appearances. Of wax dolls, perhaps the best are those by Augusta Montanari, with each individual hair set separately into the wax, in the 1850s. Other well-known makers were H. Pierotti and Charles Marsh, but few wax dolls are marked and there were many other kinds. Of the bisque dolls, the majority came from Germany, or at least their heads did, well-known names being Simon and Halbig, Heubach, and Armand Marseille; but probably most people would agree in giving the palm for appeal and elegance to the post-1874 Jumeau dolls from Paris. Less appealing but more lifelike Baby 'character' dolls from Germany were sometimes too realistic, resembling the kind of hideous baby that one hopes will 'grow out of it'.

Opening and closing eyes, by various methods, were invented earlier in the nineteenth century. There is a charming cartoon in *Punch*, c. 1880, of two little girls on a sofa:

'Says one: "My dolly can open her eyes."
Says the other: "My dolly never shuts hers."'

[120]

Doll, wax over composition, pumpkin head type, wearing typical white piqué dress with black braid embroidery 1850s

Boy doll with bisque head and short fur hair, by Ferdinand Max Schilling, early 20th century

Wax dolls that have been dearly loved and much handled show it: their noses are nearly rubbed away and all their features blurred—bisque or porcelain dolls often suffered a worse fate.

Soft cuddly toys, except for rag dolls, do not seem to have been much known before 1900. The most famous and long-lived of all is of course the Teddy Bear, called after President Theodore Roosevelt in honour of his having refrained from shooting a bearcub on a hunting trip. This bear was first made by Morris Michtom, a toymaker. The main disadvantage of soft toys was that their beady eyes became detached and were sometimes swallowed by their small owners, but later this problem was overcome. A jolly character who appeared in the 1920s was Bonzo and, shortly afterwards, came the infinitely pathetic Dismal Desmond, a black and white spotted dog. Much pity must have been lavished on this despondent animal.

A traditional toy in most nineteenth-century nurseries was the Noah's

Noah's ark with unusually realistic animals c. 1924

Ark—usually this was just a roofed box set in a hull-like base with painted doors and windows. To release the inmates, stored higgledy-piggledy inside, the whole side of the box slid out. The animals, usually roughly carved and painted, all have a marked family resemblance—the carver not apparently being familiar with the minutiae of distinctions between species and harking back to some common ancestor all the time.

Clockwork toys and automata, of an adult kind, were an offshoot of the watch-making industry and far too fragile and precious for children to play with. Wind-up toys for children developed in the late nineteenth century and by 1900 there were probably clockwork toys in most nurseries—acrobats, 'horse-less carriages', and train sets. An airship was patented in 1903 by Lehmann in Germany—although its tail fins buzzed round at great speed, this airship never actually got airborne except by being swung round on a string.

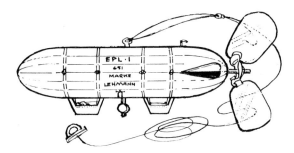

Clockwork airship, German. Patented by Lehmann in 1903

Toys Out-of-doors

Toys to be taken on walks needed to be mobile—to be pushed, pulled, rolled or pedalled along. One of the simplest and oldest forms was the hoop. In Victorian times it was mostly iron hoops that were chased up and down the park or street—a certain speed had to be kept up or the hoop fell over—in the twentieth century it was the turn of the bentwood hoop. Skipping ropes too were used before the nineteenth century had ever dawned and were another means of taking pleasurable exercise; the delights of skipping are well described by Frances Hodgson Burnett in *The Secret Garden*, when Mary, her cross-patch heroine, first tries out the, to her, new pastime. A scooter was another outdoor toy available in the 1920s for the child who was not yet old enough for a fairy cycle.

The Rocking Horse, on curved rockers until Dunkley's invented the pedestal type in the 1880s, was kept in the nursery, but in 1851 a Progressive Garden Rocking Horse was manufactured by Henry Lucas of Long Acre, London.

Small children took out with them animals on stands with wheels, which were pushed or pulled along.

[122]

BIBLIOGRAPHY

Adburgham, Alison, *Shops and Shopping* (1964).

Arnold, Janet, *The Dressmaker's Craft. In: Strata of Society* (Costume Society Conference, 1973).

Angeloglou, Maggie, *A History of Make-up* (1970).

Beeton, Isabella, *Book of Household Management* (1880 edition).

Bignell, Philippa, *Taking the Train* (1978).

Buck, Anne M., *Victorian Costume and Costume Accessories* (1961).

Cooper, Diana and Battershill, Norman, *Victorian Sentimental Jewellery* (1972).

Cunnington, C. W. and Cunnington, P., *Handbook of English Costume in the Nineteenth Century* (1966).

Dillmont, Thérèse de, *Encyclopedia of Needlework* (1880 edition).

Dunhill, Alfred, *The Pipe Book* (1969).

Ellis, C. Hamilton, *Railway Carriages in the British Isles 1830–1914* (1966).

Flower, Margaret, *Victorian Jewellery* (1967).

Gilbert, K. R., *Sewing Machines* (1970).

Groves, Sylvia, *The History of Needlework Tools and Accessories* (1973).

Haweis, Mrs, *The Art of Beauty* (1883).

Hughes, Therle, *Small Decorative Antiques* (1959).

Launert, Edmund, *Scent and Scent Bottles* (1974).

Linton, Mrs Lynn, *The Girl of the Period* (1866–67).

MacEwan, Peter, *Pharmaceutical Formulas (The Chemist & Druggist)* (1919).

Mackay, James, *Nursery Antiques* (1976).

Matthews, Leslie G., *Antiques of Perfume* (1973).

Matthews, Leslie G., *Antiques of the Pharmacy*.

Rimmel, Eugene, *The Book of Perfumes* (1865 and 1867).

Watts, M. S., *G. F. Watts* (1912).

White, Gwen, *European and American Dolls* (1966).
Williams, Neville, *Powder and Paint* (1957).
Wynne, Thomas E., *The House of Yardley* (1953).

Catalogues

Catalogue of the Army & Navy Co-operative Society Ltd (1925/6).
Official Descriptive and Illustrated Catalogue of the Great Exhibition (1851).
Sears, Roebuck Catalogue (1897).
Yesterday's Shopping (Facsimile Army & Navy Catalogue for 1907).

* * *

The many fashion magazines and other periodicals consulted include: *La Belle Assemblée (New Monthly)*, *The Englishwoman's Domestic Magazine*, *Fémina*, *Harper's Bazaar*, *The Ladies' Cabinet*, *The Queen, the Lady's Newspaper*, *Vogue*, *Weldon's*, *The World of Fashion*, *The Badminton Magazine*, *Country Life*, *Good Housekeeping*, *The Graphic*, *Illustrated London News*, *Illustrated Sporting and Dramatic News*, *Pall Mall Magazine*, *Punch*, *Strand Magazine*, *Titbits*.

ACKNOWLEDGEMENTS

The writing of this book has been made incomparably easier by the fact that I have had readily to hand, at the Hampshire County Museum Service, and especially in the collection at the Red House Museum, Christchurch, very many of the items discussed or illustrated. Thanks are therefore due to the Director of the Service, Mr K. J. Barton, for permission to use such items, as also to the Curator of the Red House Museum, John Lavender. I should like also to thank Mr and Mrs R. G. L. Rivis for allowing their Writing Desk to be used.

I am also grateful to the following for help, information or illustrations: Messrs Allen and Hanbury Ltd, Miss Pamela Clabburn, Messrs Alfred Dunhill Ltd, Dr Coiley and Mr Edgington, National Railway Museum, Mr Carpenter Turner, Mrs S. E. Messham, Wellcome Museum of the History of Medicine, Miss June Swann, Guildhall Museum, Northampton, Messrs Sheaffer, Miss Mary Sims, Miss Mary Camidge and Mrs Margaret Browne.

INDEX

Numbers in *italics* refer to illustrations

[125]